The Most Valuable Ingredient

If you weigh 70 kg (150 lbs), then 15 kg (30 lbs) are pure protein, including your hair, bones and joints, enzymes and hormones, muscles, immune system, and blood. Protein is truly the most valuable ingredient in your food – the building blocks from which your life, moods, and energy are constructed. What you eat each day must supply your body with a booster shot of protein that it can use to produce hormones, keep your immune system up and running, build up muscles, and repair cells. But is the protein you eat actually reaching the cells, where it is needed? This can only be seen by looking at your blood. The average person's blood protein level is low, resulting in fragile bones, weak muscles, a lack of red, oxygen-carrying blood cells, a listless immune system, and an unsteady psyche. People with a high blood protein level are life's winners. Nothing keeps them down.

How Much Protein Do You Have in Your Blood?

A low protein content indicates that your body is running on half power.
With a blood protein level of:

- 8 g/100 ml you feel good and are active;
- 7 g/100 ml you feel pretty good;
- 6 g/100 ml you're tired and without energy.

Ask your doctor to tell you your level.

Fill Up Your Protein Tank

When you have a lot of protein in your blood you become more alert, you concentrate better, and you're happier. So raise your protein level to the top of the normal range. To do this, you'll have to fill your body up with protein over the course of several weeks. Too much all at once won't help you, as your body will eliminate the surplus, possibly causing damage to your kidneys. So give your body only a small dose of extra protein each day, just enough to refill its empty stores. The ideal is one serving of protein every four hours, because it takes the protein four hours to pass through your kidneys and exit your body. It's a somewhat tedious process, but just consider the rewards: vitality, lust for life, and energy!

How Much Protein Does a Person Need?

At least 20 per cent of the calories you consume in a day should be in the form of protein. It is estimated that you need about 0.8 grams of protein per kilogram (2 lbs) of body weight. Therefore a person weighing 60 kg (130 lbs) has a minimum requirement of 48 grams of protein.

However, athletes, people with high-stress jobs, and people with an overall low blood protein level need more protein – up to twice as much.

Magic Amino Acids

Create energy and good moods

There are 10 amino acids that are especially important to your body – your body either can't produce these amino acids on its own or can only produce a small amount. If you don't get these 10 from your diet, the other amino acids are also rendered useless, like a house missing its beams.

Leucine Keeps You Fit

Leucine is an important building block in blood protein and tissues. This amino acid is essential for muscular stamina and physical performance. If you don't have enough, your entire body is weakened.

Isoleucine Combats Stress

Isoleucine is essential for muscular stamina and works as a brain-activating amino acid. This amino acid mainly produces neurotransmitters (chemicals that transmit messages in the brain) that protect you against stress.

Lysine Keeps You Young

As a component of collagen, lysine keeps your skin firm and protects your arteries from sclerosis. As a building block of enzymes, lysine stimulates the growth hormone (the physiological fountain of youth), which builds up muscle and burns off fat. Without lysine, there are no enzymes to fight cancer cells. Lysine is also a component of carnitine, the nutrient that channels fat to the cells, thus making fat combustion possible. Lysine strengthens your resistance to viruses and can help those suffering from a lack of drive or difficulty concentrating.

Methionine – Metabolism's Jack of All Trades

Methionine is the starting point for all protein synthesis. This amino acid is a component of carnitine, which transports fat to the cells where it is combusted. Methionine is important for the defence function (phagocytic ability) of the killer cells in the blood. It also protects the body's detoxifier – the liver.

Threonine Perks Up Weary Souls

Threonine is the key substance in the production of the endothelial relaxing factor. This means that it is essential for dilating the blood vessels and therefore for the flow of blood through the body, heart, and brain. A deficiency may result in constricted blood vessels, fatigue, and even heart trouble.

Phenylalanine Lifts Spirits and Stops Hunger

This amino acid is a basic material for mood elevating hormones such as norepinephrine, ACTH, dopamine, and endorphins. Phenylalanine helps relieve depression and build self-esteem. It's also used as a pain remedy for arthritis, rheumatism, and muscular pain. In the intestines, phenylalanine helps regulate cholecystokinin, the hormone that signals to the brain when you're full.

Tryptophan Relaxes

The body uses tryptophan to produce melatonin, the fountain-of-youth hormone, as well as serotonin, the chief hormone for inner peace, equanimity, and happiness. When you're under stress, anxious, or having difficulty sleeping, or if you want to quit smoking, take an extra helping of tryptophan. A deficiency can result in depression and even psychosis.

Valine Peps Up Nerves and Your Immune System

Valine promotes the healthy functioning of your nervous system and aids in the production of haemoglobin, the red blood pigment that transports revitalizing oxygen to all your cells. Valine is also important for building up an active immune system.

Histidine Puts the Wind in Your Sails

Histidine is also needed for producing the oxygen-carrying red haemoglobin. In other words, the more histidine you have, the better you perform, both physically and mentally. Histidine regulates cell growth and regeneration. The cells' tiny power plants, the mitochondria, require this amino acid for transporting oxygen and, therefore, for producing power.

Taurine Keeps You Thin

This protein material is important for over-eaters and food lovers because taurine can increase fat combustion fourfold. And taurine also detoxifies the liver whenever it suffers a toxic overload (such as from alcohol). This amino acid also blocks the unpleasant effects of caffeine by slowing down your pulse.

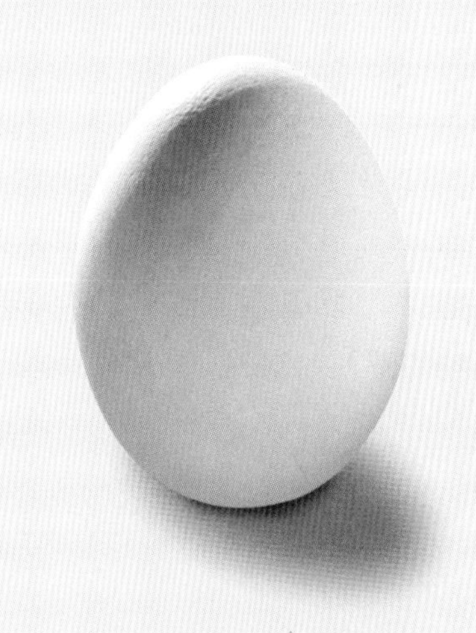

Eat Protein with Little or No Fat

Stay fit and trim

Is too much protein a bad thing? Certainly "too much" of anything is bad, even too much oxygen. We can't live without oxygen, but when there's too much it becomes toxic. The question is, how much is too much? Your body contains about 15 kg (30 lbs) of protein. Every day you lose a handful of it, from 50 to 100 g (2 to 4 oz), and every day you have to replenish it.

Most people have a low protein level even when they eat a huge amount of protein, usually in the form of meat. The problem is that the protein on your plate never reaches the places where you need it most – the places in your body where the tiny protein building blocks, the amino acids, work to raise your spirits, repair cells, mobilize your immune system, build up your muscles, and get your power hormones moving. And why doesn't it reach its destination? First of all, because you lack the vital nutrients required for digesting protein. Nutritious protein is lying inert in your intestines, bloating you, and causing allergies.

Secondly, because you eat protein with fat. If you really want to fill up your tank with protein power, you need to eat protein on its own, without the fat. Fat prevents the valuable amino acids from participating in metabolism, starting in your intestines. Fat hinders peristalsis, the movement of the intestines. It takes only a minimal amount of fat to delay the absorption of protein into the bloodstream by several hours. The amino acids barely trickle into your bloodstream and can't reach the cells fast enough or in large enough quantities to do you any good. Unless the correct amount of protein is made available all at once, your body can never activate sufficient quantities of hormones and neurotransmitters, elevate your brain to a state of euphoria, render your thoughts crystal-clear, fill you full of self-confidence, or help you to achieve your highest level of performance.

Where can you find protein with little or no fat? Valuable sources include tender fish, lean poultry, cottage cheese, yogurt, and other low-fat dairy products, as well as legumes. But since you can't have a plateful of these foods every four hours, I suggest that you also use a high-quality protein powder, preferably in combination with fruit or vegetables. Fruits and vegetables provide the nutrients you need to transport the protein to the 70 billion cells in your body, making you thin and happy, healthy and fit, stress-proof and creative, youthful and beautiful.

Protein Powder from the Healthfood Shop

Because protein is almost always combined with fat, you can seldom consume enough protein to fill up your empty stores without simultaneously broadening your hips. So go to the health food store and buy protein without fat. A good protein powder is an excellent means of raising your blood protein level. After only a few days you will see – or rather feel – that you have more power, your thoughts are clearer, and your mood simply couldn't be better.

Note: If you fill up your tank with protein powder, you also need to drink a lot of liquid – at least 3 litres (6 pints) a day.

A Good Powder

A protein powder from the healthfood shop is good quality if it contains 60 per cent animal protein (usually from egg whites and milk) and 40 per cent plant protein (frequently soy). In addition, an extra serving of carnitine in the protein powder will help you lose weight. Added vitamins and minerals will ensure an efficient protein metabolism and help you fill up your empty vital nutrient tanks.

Protein Powder as a Fitness Drink

One or two of the fitness drinks from pages 12 to 58 every day, along with a healthy low-sugar, low-fat diet, will help you to fill up your empty tanks.

Naturally, you could simply dissolve the protein powder in water or low-fat milk. But you also need to make sure you eat some fruit or vegetables, because these foods contain the active ingredients that render the protein biologically active in your body. So why not combine them, as we have done in these recipes, especially when they taste so delicious?

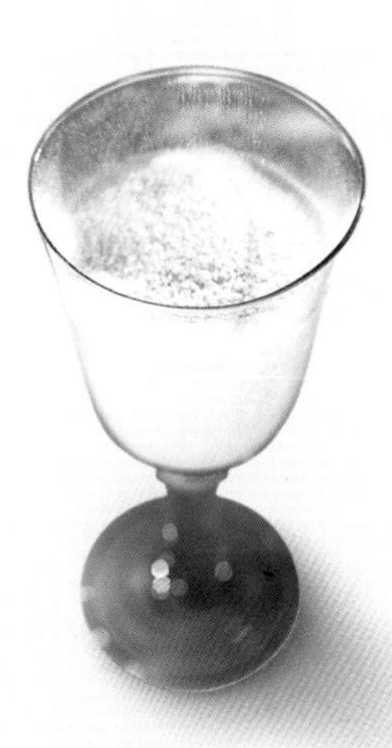

Power Week

Losing weight with protein drinks

You can lose 500 g (1 lb) a day by stimulating the fat-burning process with exercise, protein, and vital nutrients. A deficiency in these three elements is the sole reason why so many people today are overweight. No diet can help you achieve long-term weight loss. On the contrary, if you starve yourself, your body will attack your muscles and consume the only organs that burn fat. But you can prevent this by running for 30 minutes every day – easily, without stress, and with a smile – and by consuming protein, which prevents your body from breaking down muscle mass.

Protein is also responsible for fat being sucked out of the fat cells and burned. Especially when you're trying to lose weight, your body needs protein that it can invest in muscles and fat-burning hormones, such as the growth hormone HGH that builds muscles and melts fat.

Another important factor is vital nutrients. We would all have a higher fat metabolism if our diet contained enough vital nutrients. Vitamin C boosts fat combustion,as do vitamin B6, magnesium, iodine, chromium, and selenium.

How to Melt Away the Fat

Prepare: Buy a good pair of running shoes and a pulse monitor. Check with your doctor whether it's safe for you to run and diet.

Run: Run 30 minutes every morning and evening, keeping your pulse below 140.

Consume protein: Drink three fitness drinks per day. For suggestions, see the next page.

Drink: Drink 3 litres (6 pints) of water each day. Tea and vegetable juices are also permitted, but don't drink alcohol.

Consider a supplement: Choose a good multivitamin and mineral preparation. This will stimulate fat metabolism, fill up empty stores, and prevent deficiencies.

Fill up on fruit: In addition to the fruit drinks, you can also feast on pure fruit – as much as you want and whatever you want. The best are the tropical fruits and any fruits that are in season.

Maintain your weight: Once you've lost enough weight, continue to run 30 minutes every day. If you can maintain your weight for three to six months, you've made it!

PLAN FOR THE WEEK

Monday

❋ Strawberry and Pineapple Mix ❋ Melon Shake ❋ Tomato and Avocado Drink

Tuesday

❋ Papaya and Orange Shake ❋ Cherry Buttermilk Drink ❋ Icy Cucumber Dill Drink

Wednesday

❋ Mango and Coconut Drink ❋ Chocolate and Pear Shake ❋ Carrot and Herb Shake

Thursday

❋ Kiwi and Grapefruit Drink with Mint ❋ Apricot and Almond Shake ❋ Mango and Carrot Mix

Friday

❋ Apple and Elderberry Drink ❋ CitrusButtermilk Flip ❋ Spicy Vegetable Shake

Saturday

❋ Berry Smoothie ❋ Banana and Yogurt Drink ❋ Kiwi and Avocado Mix

Sunday

❋ Peach Melba Cocktail ❋ C-Packed Blueberry Shake ❋ Celeriac and Spinach Flip

Six reasons why it's worth switching on the blender

1. Protein power: Your protein tanks are empty. Replenish your stores with fitness drinks.
2. Fat-burning power: Fitness drinks supply all the vital nutrients with few calories.
3: Muscle power: Protein prevents your body from depriving your immune system in order to build up your muscles.
4. Brain boosting: It's best to fill up your empty nutrient stores in the morning. Your brain will then have an ample supply to support serenity, creativity, and flashes of genius.
5. Cell rejuvenation: These drinks contain all the nutrients your 70 billion cells need to renew themselves again and again.
6: Good mood material: Protein and nutrients from fruit or vegetables provide the basis for the happy messengers. Your body starts producing more serotonin and endorphins.

Seasonal Fruits Calendar

Fruits with enzymes are best

In Praise of Fruit

Do you eat fruit five times a day? If you answered no, you should start doing so now. Nothing provides you with more vital nutrients and healthy energy than fresh fruit from nature's garden.

Fruit nourishes your thoughts because its fructose provides steady reinforcements for the brain without putting stress on your blood sugar level. Vital nutrients in fruit help to prevent fatigue, sharpen your concentration, and raise your spirits through the production of hormones.

Fruit keeps you thin. Its vitamin C, minerals, and phytochemicals boost fat metabolism and clean out the body via the kidneys. Fruit's fibre sets sluggish digestion in motion and carries toxins out of the intestines.

Fruit is medicine and has been used as such for millennia. Its vital nutrients strengthen your organs, aid in blood production, steady your nerves, and keep your digestive glands up and running. Fruit helps lower your blood pressure and keep your blood fat values low. It fortifies your immune system, purifies your intestines, cleans out all your blood vessels, and strengthens connective tissue in your skin and blood vessels. Fruit protects you against cancer, heart attacks, and strokes, mitigates asthma symptoms, and slows down the ageing process. It helps you fall asleep and works against migraines. It strengthens your bones, raises your libido, and makes your hair shine. One thing's for certain: there's a fruit for every complaint – you just have to pluck it five times a day.

A tip for fitness and eternal youth: every day, make yourself a large bowl of fruit salad using whatever fruits are in season.

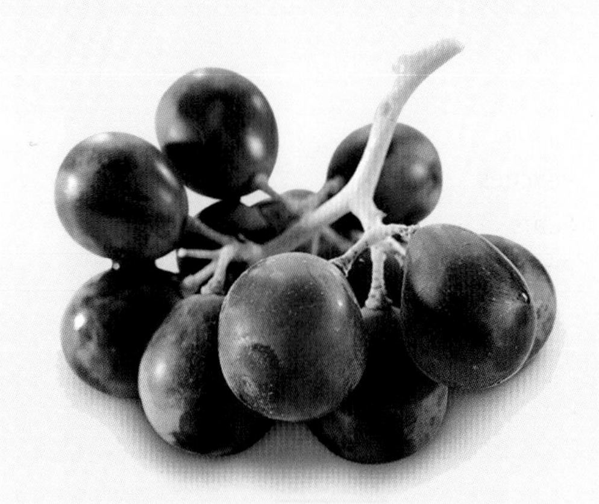

Fruits Calendar

	Jan	Feb	March	April	May	June	July	Aug	Sept	Oct	Nov	Dec
Apples	*	*	*	*	*	*	*	*	*	*	*	*
Apricots					*	*	*	*	*			
Avocados	*	*	*	*	*	*	*	*	*	*	*	*
Bananas	*	*	*	*	*	*	*	*	*	*	*	*
Blackberries						*	*	*	*	*		
Blackcurrants						*	*	*				
Blueberries						*	*	*	*			
Cherries					*	*	*	*				
Dates	*	*	*	*	*	*	*	*	*	*	*	*
Elderberries									*	*	*	
Figs (fresh)	*	*	*	*	*	*	*	*	*	*	*	*
Gooseberries					*	*	*	*				
Grapefruit	*	*	*	*	*	*	*	*	*	*	*	*
Grapes	*	*					*	*	*	*	*	*
Kiwis	*	*	*	*	*	*	*	*	*	*	*	*
Mangoes	*	*	*	*	*	*	*	*	*	*	*	*
Melon	*	*	*	*	*	*	*	*	*	*	*	*
Oranges	*	*	*	*	*	*	*	*	*	*	*	*
Papaya	*	*	*	*	*	*	*	*	*	*	*	*
Peaches	*	*	*	*	*	*	*	*	*			
Pears	*	*	*	*	*	*	*	*	*	*	*	*
Pineapple	*	*	*	*	*	*	*	*	*	*	*	*
Plums	*	*	*	*	*	*	*	*	*	*		
Raspberries						*	*	*	*			
Strawberries	*	*	*	*	*	*	*	*			*	*
Tangerines	*	*	*							*	*	*

* These symbols indicate the months when the fruit is available.

* These symbols indicate the high season for each fruit.

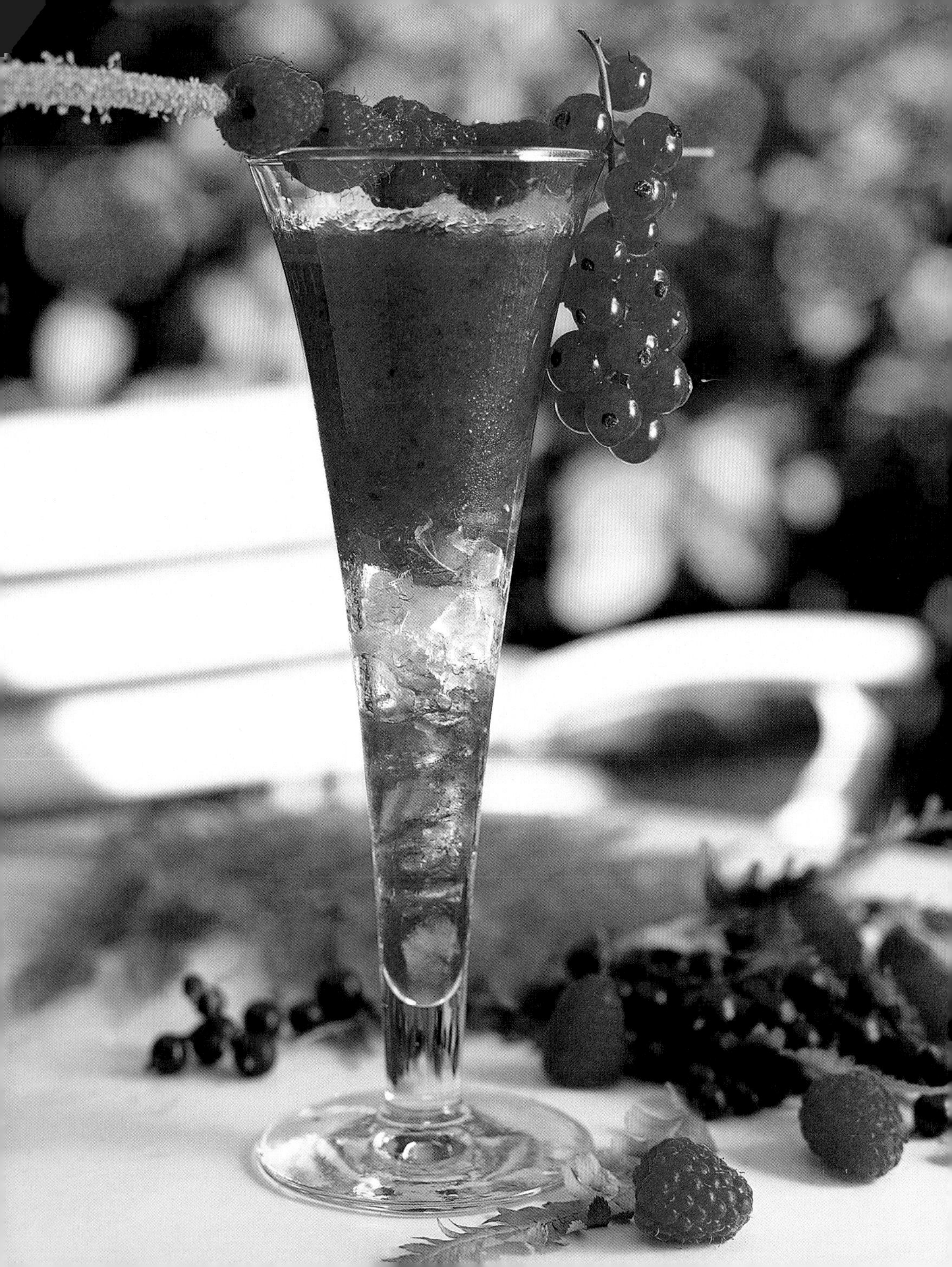

Berry Smoothie

Soothing fitness drink

Rinse the berries, remove their stems, and keep a few berries for garnish. Put the rest in a blender. Add the maple syrup and orange juice and blend thoroughly for 15 seconds.

Cut the frozen banana into small pieces. Add the banana, protein powder, and water to the blender and blend thoroughly for 15 seconds more.

Pour the mixture into a frosted cocktail glass. Thread the reserved berries on to a cocktail skewer and lie it across the top of the glass. Serve the drink with a straw.

Tip: To frost the cocktail glass, place it in the refrigerator or freezer for several hours ahead of time, or fill the glass with crushed ice and let it stand briefly.

Serves 1:
80 g (3 oz) mixed berries
2 tsp maple syrup
2 tbsp orange juice
1 medium banana, frozen
2 tbsp protein powder
125 ml (4 fl oz) cold mineral water

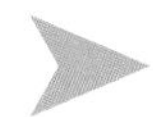

Berries

In Asia, these small fruits are used as a folk remedy. They're jam-packed with vitamins and minerals.. Berries' essential oils, pigments, and tannins fill you with energy, calm your nerves, and leave you fit and relaxed. Their flavones protect you from cancer. In addition to boosting your metabolism, berries fortify your immune system, strengthen your heart, aid your kidneys in detoxifying your body, and help prevent rheumatism, arthritis, and diabetes.

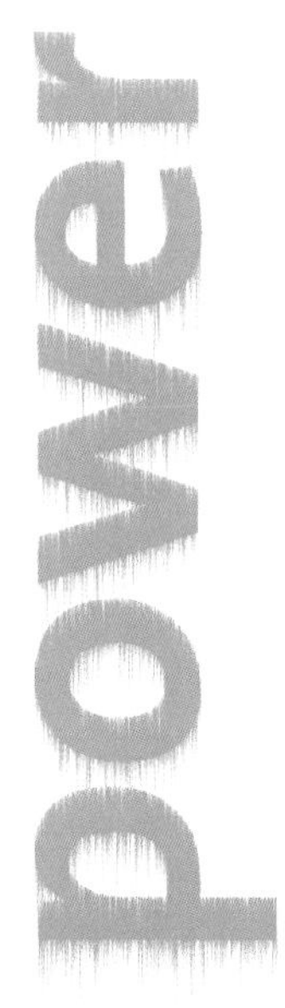

Mango and Coconut Drink

Tropical power for your cells

Peel and dice the mango. Set aside three nice mango cubes for garnish and place the remaining pieces in the blender.

Serves 1:
1 piece mango (100 g (4 oz))
1 lime
2 tsp brown sugar
50 ml (2 fl oz) cold unsweetened coconut milk
2 tbsp protein powder
125 ml (4 fl oz) cold unfiltered apple juice
1–2 tbsp grated coconut

Peel a spiral-shaped strip of zest from the lime and set it aside. Squeeze the lime juice and add it to the blender with the sugar and coconut milk. Blend thoroughly for 15 seconds. Add the protein powder and apple juice. Blend thoroughly for 10 seconds more.

Moisten the rim of a large glass with water, turn the glass upside-down, and dip the rim into the grated coconut. Place ice cubes in the glass and pour the contents of the blender over the top. Thread the reserved mango cubes on to a cocktail skewer and lay them across the rim of the glass. Garnish with the lime zest. Serve the drink with a straw.

Coconut

This cannonball of minerals (mainly magnesium, iron, sodium, and selenium) protects your heart, calms your nerves, and maintains your stomach and intestines. This exotic fruit also supplies valuable plant protein.. Coconut is the ideal fruit for combating stress. In south-east Asia it's prescribed for heartburn and gastritis.

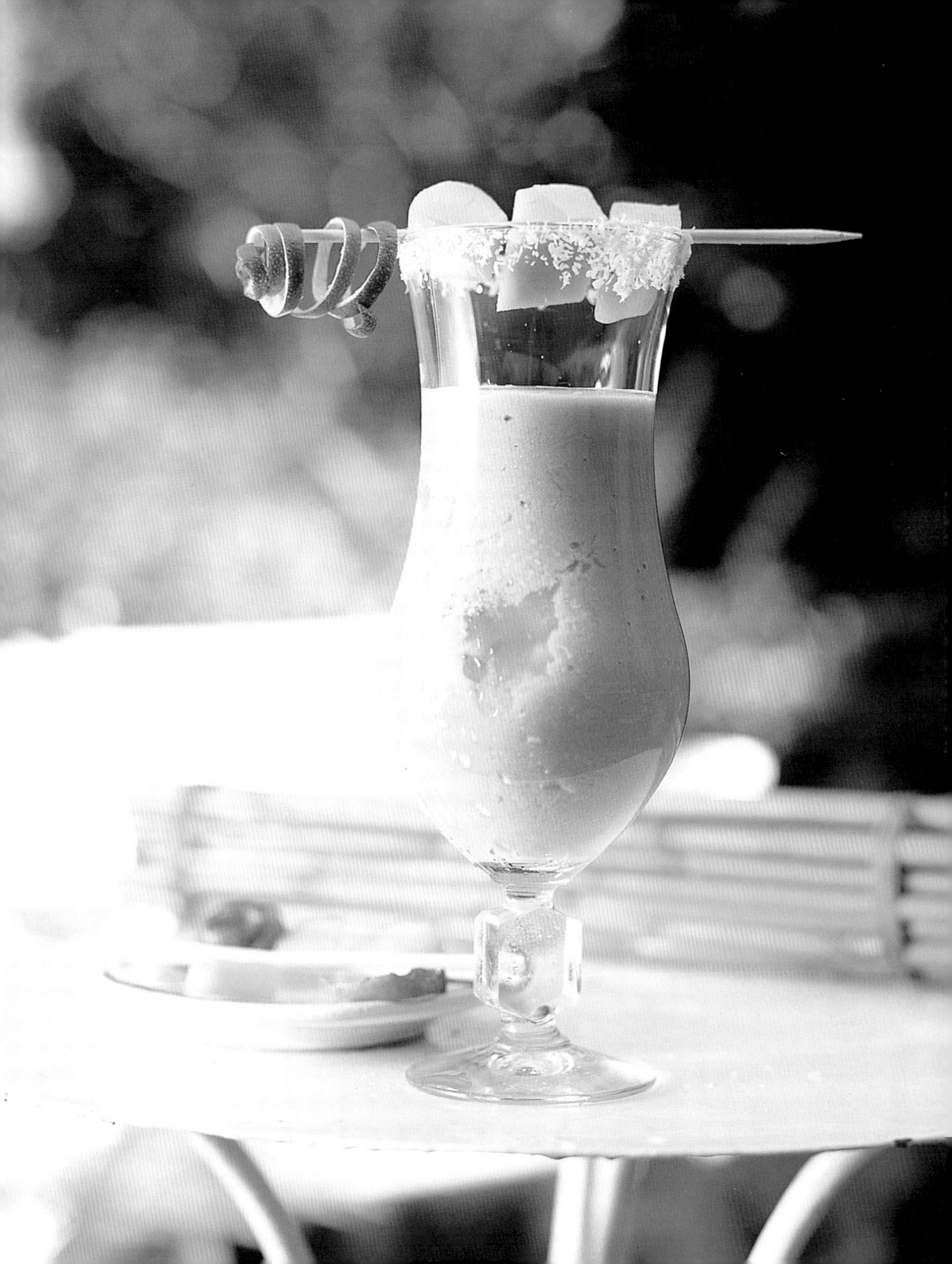

Strawberry and Pineapple Mix

The skinny drink

Wash the strawberries and set one aside for garnish. Hull the remaining strawberries and cut them into quarters.

Serves 1:
75 g (3 oz) strawberries
2 tsp lemon juice
1 tsp floral honey
150 ml (5 fl oz) cold pineapple juice
2 tbsp protein powder

Put the strawberries, lemon juice, honey, and half of the pineapple juice in a blender and blend thoroughly for 15 seconds.

Add the protein powder and the remaining pineapple juice and blend for 10 seconds more.

Pour the mixture into a tall glass. Cut part-way into the reserved strawberry and place it on the rim of the glass for garnish. Serve the drink with a straw.

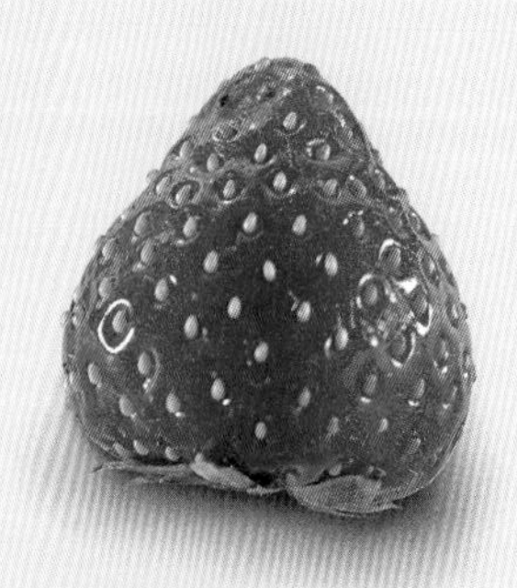

Strawberries

Strawberries make you thin while you eat. These small red balls of fitness provide more fat-burning vitamin C than lemons and have almost no calories: 100 g (4 oz) contain fewer than 40 calories. Strawberries' super fibre pectin lowers your cholesterol level and another 300 ingredients make them precious medicine. Strawberries aid digestion, clean mucous membranes, reduce fevers, serve as a diuretic, boost metabolism, and even send bacteria scurrying.

power

Papaya and Orange Shake

Morning dose of fitness

Peel the papaya and remove the seeds. Cut a wedge and set it aside for garnish. Dice the remaining papaya and place it in a blender. Add the lime juice, honey, and half of the orange juice and blend thoroughly for 15 seconds.

Add the protein powder and the remaining orange juice and blend for 10 seconds more.

Place two ice cubes in a large glass and pour in the contents of the blender. Cut part-way into the reserved papaya wedge and lime slice and place them on the rim of the glass. Serve the drink with a straw.

Serves 1:

120 g (4 oz) ripe papaya
1 tbsp lime juice
1 tsp floral honey
125 ml (4 fl oz) cold freshly squeezed orange juice
2 tbsp protein powder
1 lime slice

power

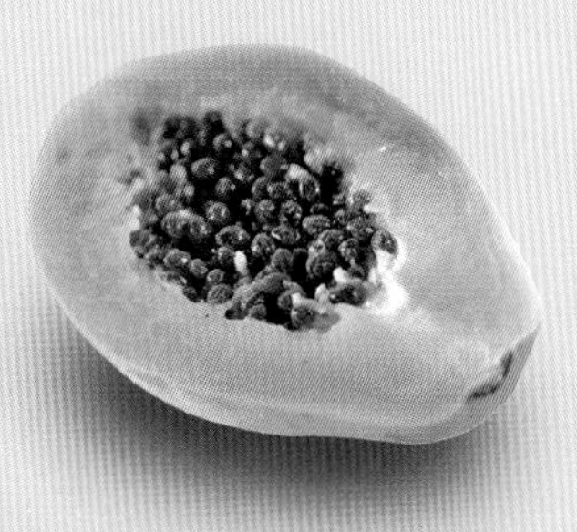

Papaya

There are many reasons to start your day with papaya. It stimulates your digestion and pampers your body with beta carotene, the nutrient that protects your cells against premature ageing. Papaya's calcium and potassium content arm you against stress.

Kiwi and Grapefruit Drink with Mint

Reinforce your immune system

Set aside one kiwi slice for garnish. Peel the remaining kiwi, dice it, and put it in a blender. Set aside one small mint sprig. Remove the remaining mint leaves from the stems and cut them into fine strips. Add the mint leaves, lemon juice, maple syrup, and half of the grapefruit juice to the blender. Blend thoroughly for 15 seconds.

Add the protein powder and the remaining juice and blend for 10 seconds more.

Put ice cubes in a large glass and pour the kiwi mixture over the top. Cut part-way into the reserved kiwi slice and place it on the rim of the glass. Garnish with the reserved mint sprig. Serve with a straw.

Serves 1:

1 kiwi (about 100 g (4 oz))
2 small sprigs fresh mint
2 tsp lemon juice
2 tsp maple syrup
150 ml (5 fl oz) cold grapefruit juice
2 tbsp protein powder

power

Kiwi

This exotic green fruit has three times the vitamin C of citrus fruit. It also contains the enzyme actinidin, which helps the digestive system break down protein. Combined with grapefruit, kiwi provides your immune system with an extra dose of power.

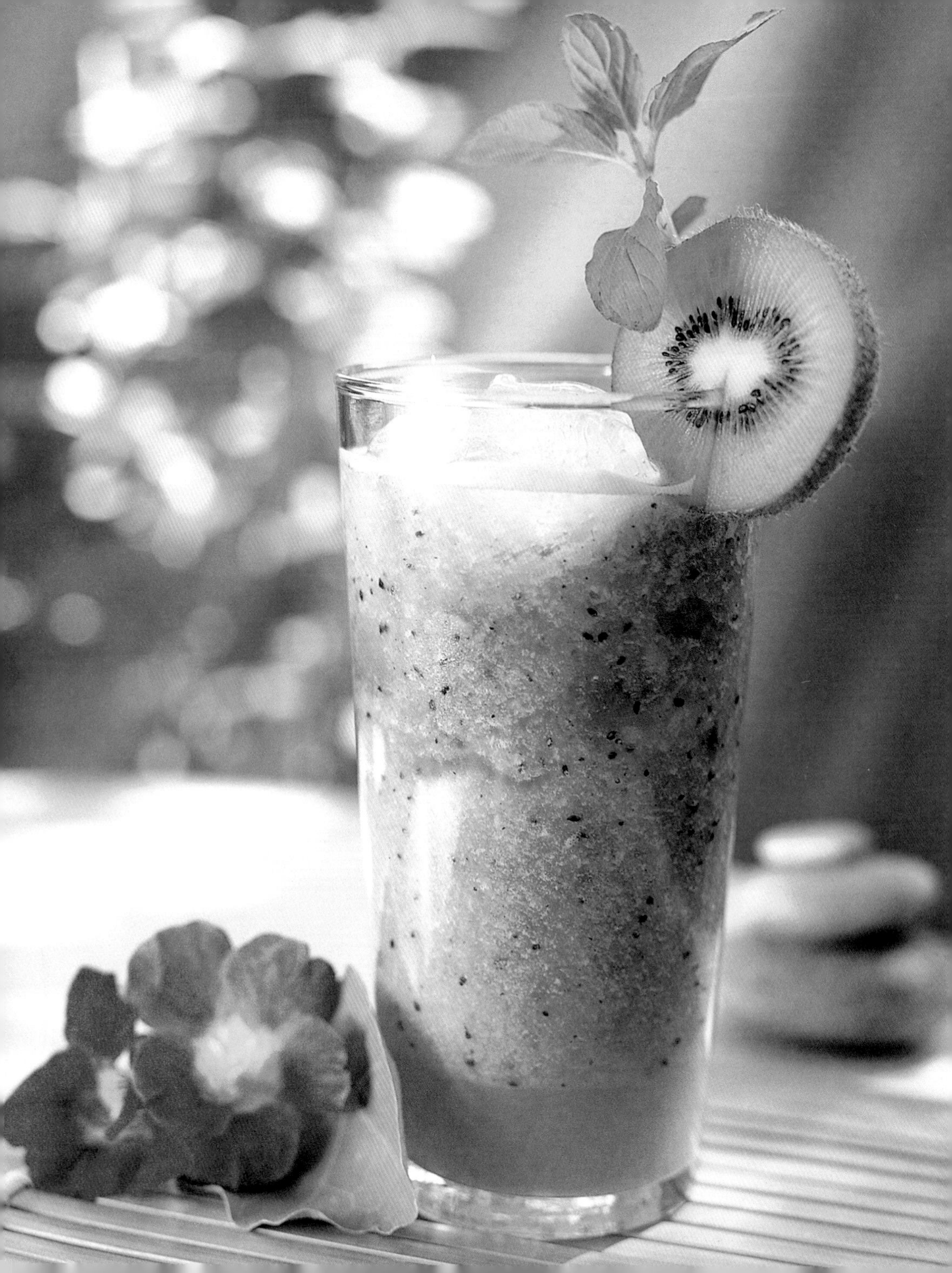

Peach Melba Cocktail

A cool cup

Wash the raspberries, sort them, and set aside four or five berries for garnish. Put the remaining raspberries and 1 teaspoon of the maple syrup in a blender and purée the berries. Pour the berry purée into a large glass.

Serves 1:
80 g (3 oz) fresh raspberries
2 tsp maple syrup
1 ripe peach (100 g (4 oz))
2 tsp lemon juice
2 tbsp protein powder
100 ml (3 1/2 fl oz) cold mineral water
1 scoop vanilla frozen yogurt

Plunge the peach into a pan of boiling water for a few seconds to loosen the skin, then plunge it into a bowl of iced water. Remove the peach peel with a small knife. Cut the fruit in half, remove the stone, and cut the fruit into pieces. Put the peach, lemon juice, the remaining maple syrup, the protein powder, and half of the mineral water in the blender. Blend thoroughly for 15 seconds.

Add the remaining mineral water and blend for 10 seconds more. Carefully pour the peach mixture over the puréed raspberries. Top with the frozen yogurt and garnish with the whole raspberries. Serve immediately with a spoon and a fat straw.

Peaches

With their abundance of aromatics, these sweet, juicy fruits woo every palate. Peaches also beguile your nerves with B vitamins, satisfy your immune system with vitamin C, and pamper your bones with a concentrated charge of calcium.

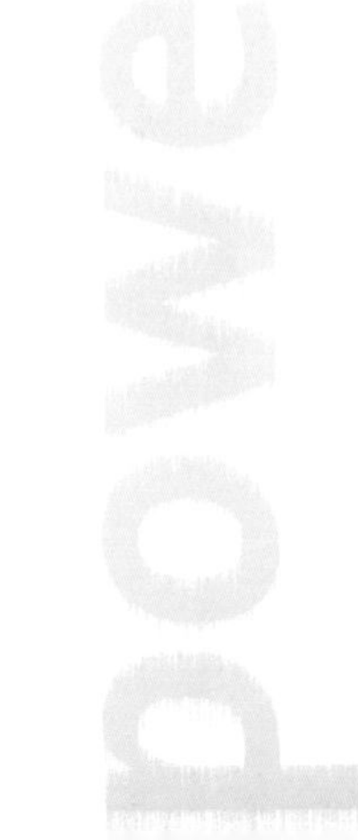

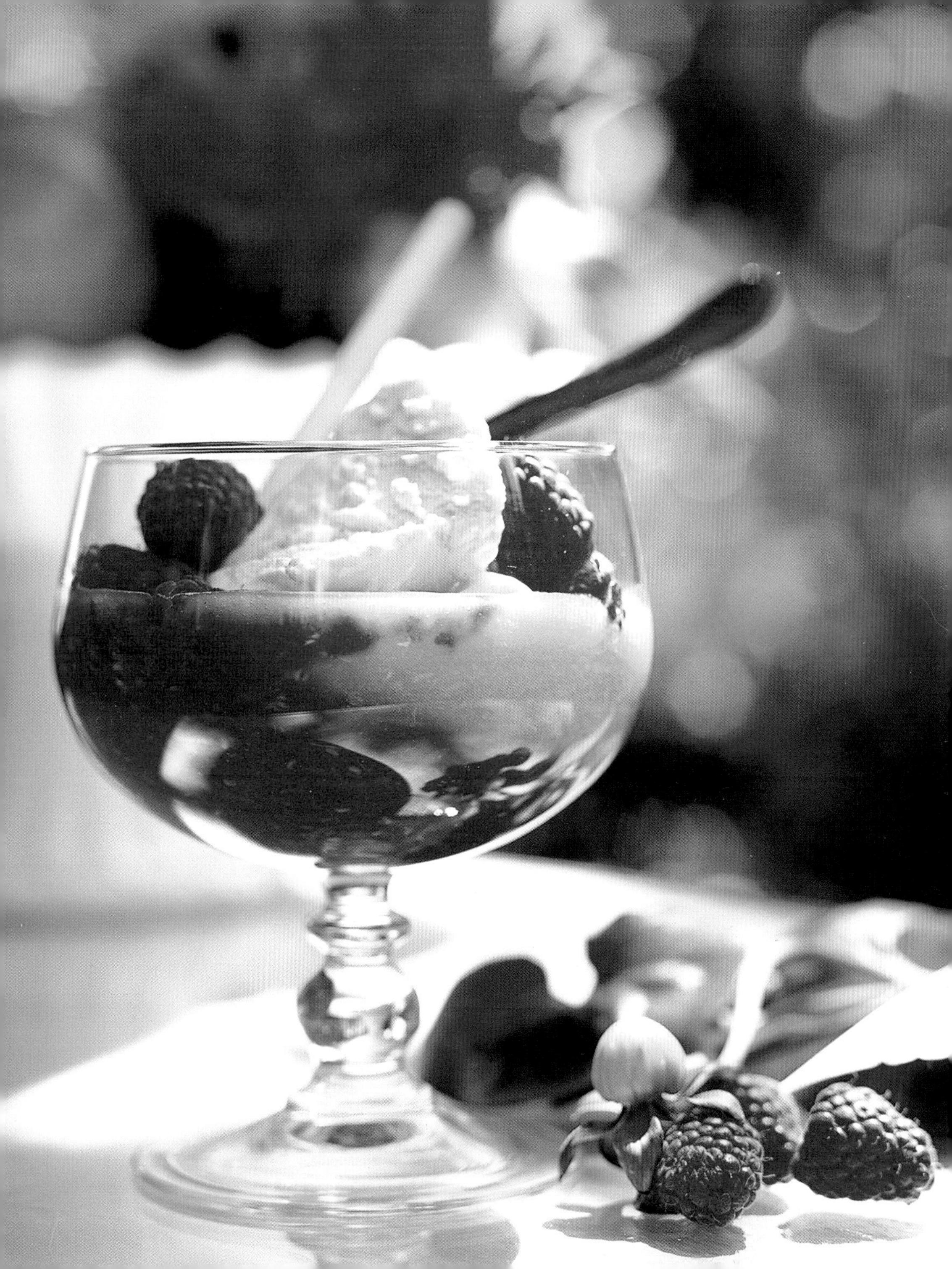

Kiwi and Avocado Mix

Green fitness cocktail

Peel the avocado and chop the flesh, removing the stone. Put the avocado in a blender and drizzle with the lemon juice.

Serves 1:
50 g (2 oz) ripe avocado
2 tbsp lemon juice
1 kiwi (about 120 g (4 oz))
1 tsp brown sugar
125 ml (4 fl oz) cold mineral water
2 tbsp protein powder
1 sprig fresh lemon balm

Set aside one kiwi slice for garnish. Peel the remaining kiwi, chop it coarsely, and add it to the blender along with the sugar and half the mineral water. Blend thoroughly for 15 seconds.

Add the protein powder and the remaining mineral water and blend thoroughly for 10 seconds more.

Put ice cubes in a large glass and pour the avocado mixture over the top. Cut part-way into the reserved kiwi slice and place on the rim of the glass. Garnish with the lemon balm.

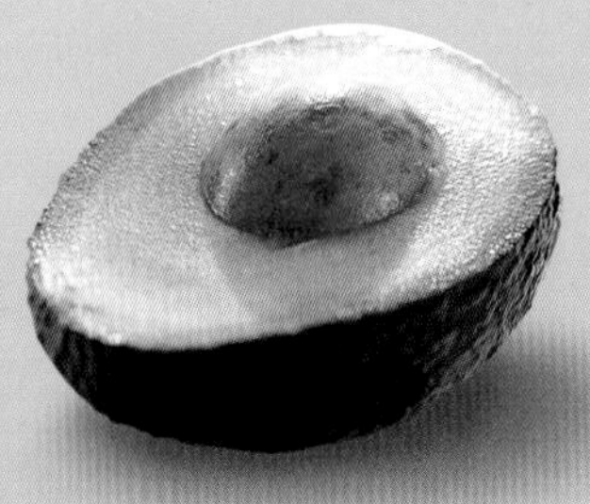

Avocados

Avocados provide unsaturated fatty acids that are essential to health. They moisturize your skin, lubricate cell walls, and fortify your nerves. Along with the finest oil, they supply nutritious protein. Avocados' true magic is in their mannoheptulose, a unique carbohydrate that lowers the blood sugar level. Eating avocados will make you feel alive, focused, and alert. And the vitamin E in avocados will also protect your heart.

power

White Fruit Cocktail

Joyfully refreshing

Peel the orange and lemon slices, and chop the fruit. Peel the apple, quarter, remove the core, and cut the fruit into small pieces. Wash and dice the peach. Put the prepared fruit and half of the grape juice in a blender and blend thoroughly for 15 seconds.

Add the protein powder, cinnamon, and the remaining juice and blend for 10 seconds more.

Put ice cubes in a large glass and pour the fruit mixture over the top. Wash the grapes, remove the stems, thread them on to a small cocktail skewer, and lay it across the rim of the glass. Serve the drink with a fat straw.

Serves 1:

1 orange slice
1 lemon slice
1/4 tart apple
1/4 peach
150 ml (5 fl oz) cold white grape juice
2 tbsp protein powder
2 pinches ground cinnamon
3 small seedless grapes

Apples

Apples provide you with several hundred nutrients. They stimulate digestion, drive away bacteria, pep up your immune system, and keep you thin. Organic acids help your liver to detoxify and pectin lowers your cholesterol level, as well as protecting your intestines and blood vessels. Start off your day with an apple and end it with one too. Apples contain nutrients that wake you up in the morning and relax you at night.

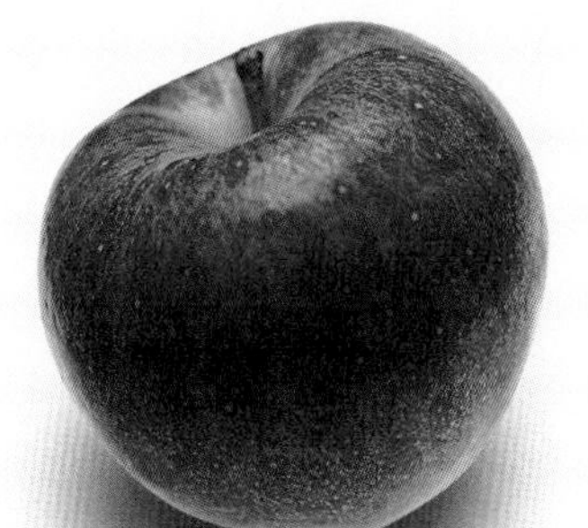

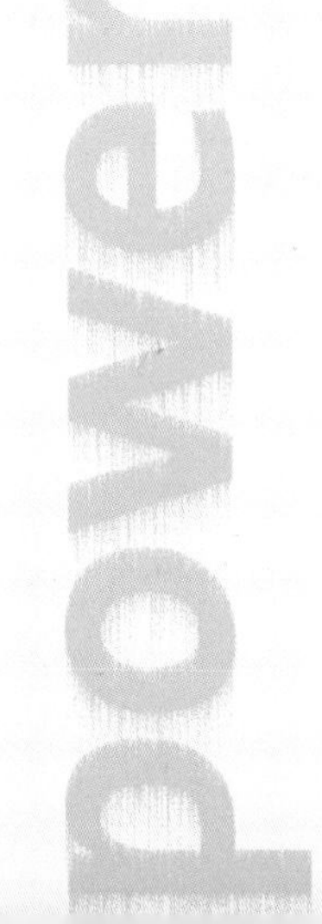

Apple and Elderberry Drink

Sweet medicine

Wash the apple and set aside a nice wedge for garnish. Peel and core the remaining apple, cut the fruit into small pieces, and put it in a blender.

Serves 1:
75 g (3 oz) tart apple
2 tsp lemon juice
2 tsp floral honey
75 ml (3 fl oz) cold unfiltered apple juice
2 tbsp protein powder
60 ml (2 fl oz) cold elderberry juice
1 sprig fresh lemon balm

Add the lemon juice, honey, and apple juice to the blender and blend the contents thoroughly for 15 seconds.

Add the protein powder and elderberry juice and blend vigorously for 10 seconds more.

Put ice cubes in a large glass and pour the mixture over the top. Place the apple wedge on the rim of the glass. Garnish the drink with lemon balm and serve with a straw.

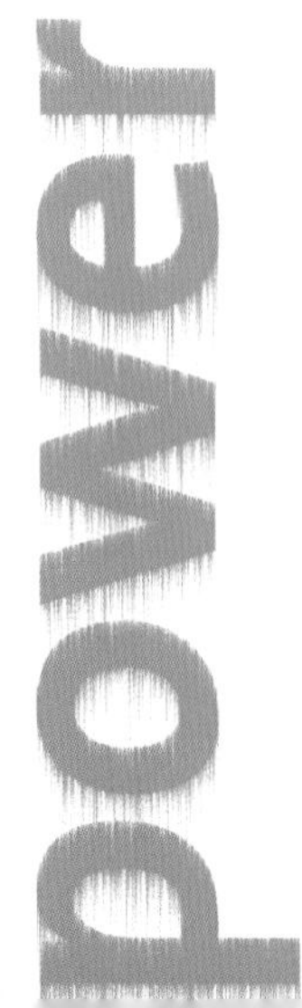

Elderberries

Elderberries contain the trace element selenium, which gives you a joyful serenity, protects all your cells, and counteracts heavy metals. In addition, elderberry juice is better for treating colds than the popular hot lemon juice.

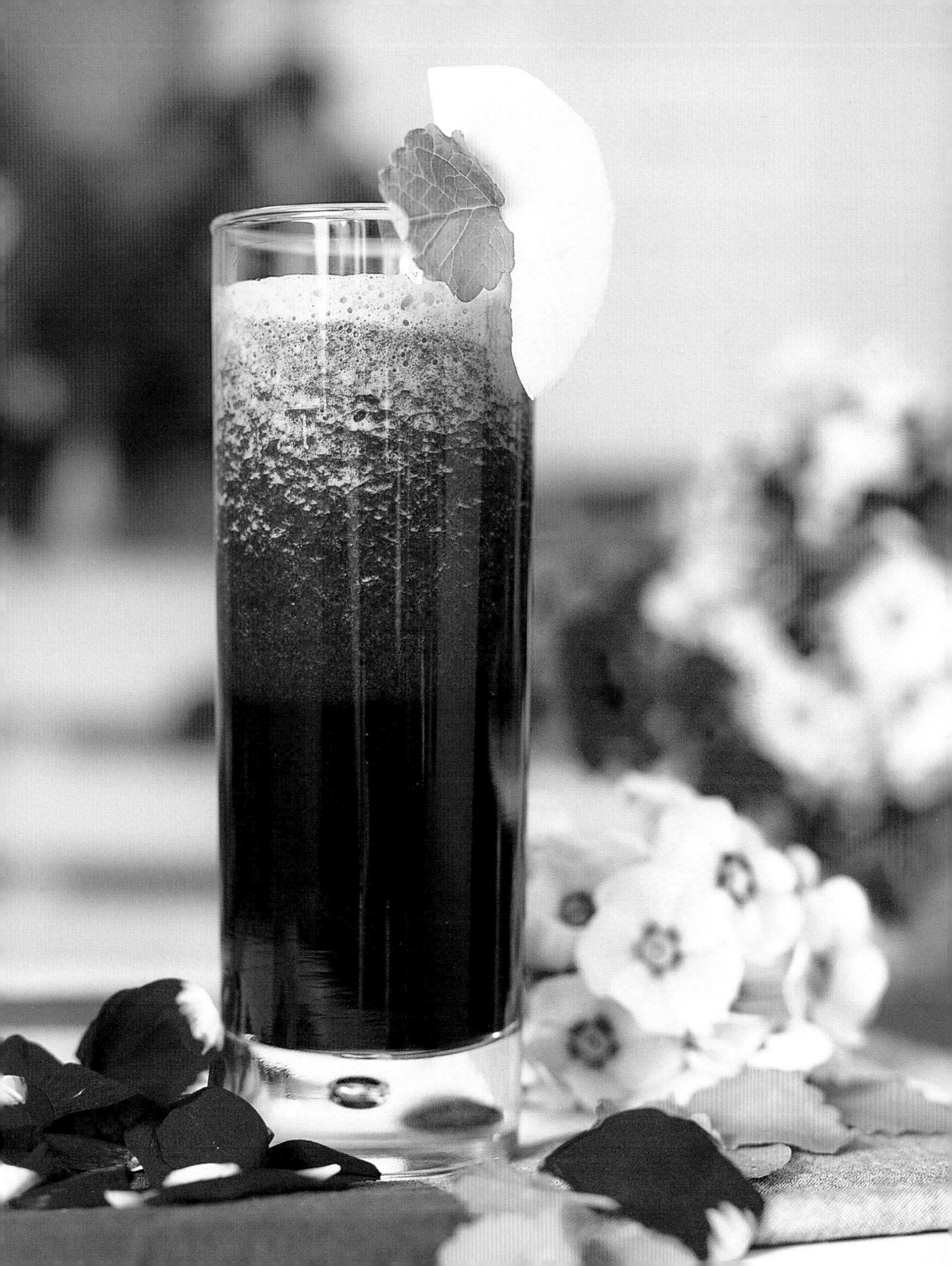

Persimmon and Orange Drink

An autumn cocktail

Wash the persimmon, cut it in half, and set aside a nice wedge for garnish. Peel the remaining persimmon, remove the core, and chop the fruit. Put the persimmon, lime juice, and apple juice concentrate in a blender. Add the vanilla extract and half of the orange juice. Blend the mixture thoroughly for 15 seconds.

Serves 1:
1/2 fully ripe Hachiya persimmon (125 g (5 oz))
1 tbsp lime juice
2 tsp apple juice concentrate
1 tsp vanilla extract
150 ml (5 fl oz) freshly squeezed orange juice
2 tbsp protein powder
1 sprig fresh lemon balm

Add the protein powder and the remaining juice and blend for 10 seconds more.

Pour the mixture into a large glass. Cut part-way into the persimmon wedge and place it on the rim of the glass. Garnish the drink with the lemon balm sprig and serve with a straw.

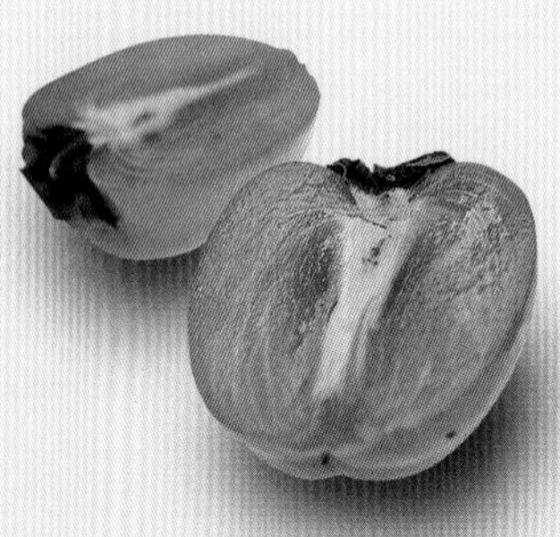

Persimmons

These fist-sized sweet, orange berries taste like a cross between a tomato and an apricot. They're the ideal brain food. Each contains up to 20 per cent glucose, an instant burst of energy for the brain. Like all tropical fruits, persimmons are chock-full of vitamins and are especially rich in skin-protecting vitamin A.

power

Blackcurrant and Banana Shake

Power for your nerves

Peel the banana. Cut out a diagonal slice and set it aside for garnish. Chop the remaining banana coarsely and put it in a blender along with the lemon juice, honey, and half of the blackcurrant juice. Blend thoroughly for 15 seconds. Add the protein powder and the remaining juice and blend for 10 seconds more.

Put ice cubes in a tall glass and pour the mixture over the top. Cut part-way into the banana slice and place it on the rim of the glass. Serve the drink with a straw.

Serves 1:
1/2 medium banana (about 100 g (4 oz))
1 tbsp lemon juice
2 tsp floral honey
150 ml (5 fl oz) cold blackcurrant juice
2 tbsp protein powder

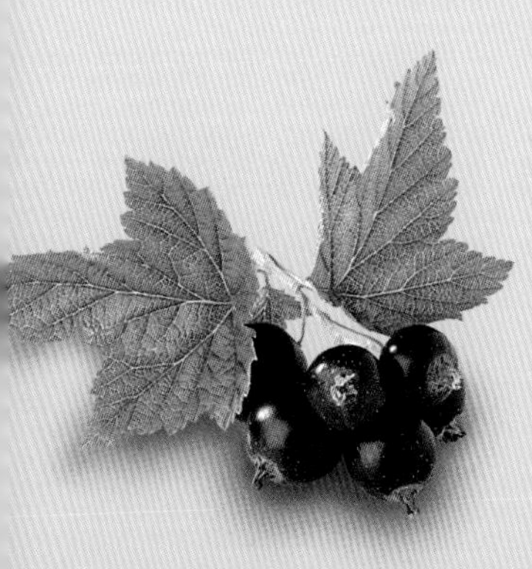

Blackcurrants

A single blackcurrant supplies no less than 2 mg of vitamin C. This power vitamin works in every cell as a biological catalyst for countless enzymatic processes, including in fat combustion, in the immune system, and in the production of hard connective tissue. It also gives you firm skin and elastic blood vessels. Above all, during stressful times, blackcurrant juice steadies your nerves. And what makes these sour berries even sweeter is that they contain pantothenic acid, the vitamin that keeps your hair from turning grey.

power

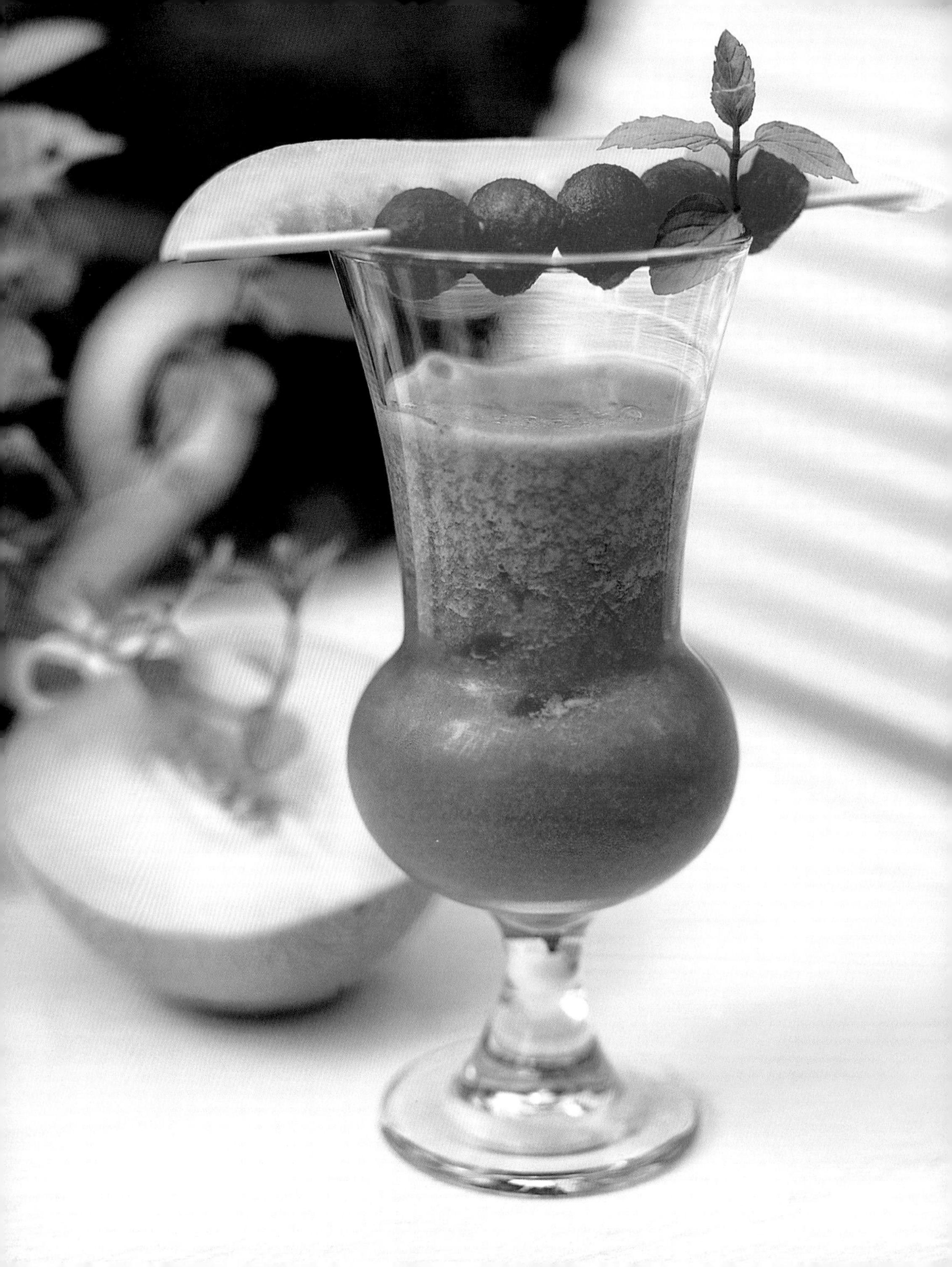

Melon Shake

A cocktail for your heart

Using a melon baller, remove five nice balls from the melon. Set aside the melon balls and a cut a wedge of melon for garnish. Peel the remaining melon, remove the seeds, cut the flesh into pieces, and put them in a blender.

Rinse the mint and set aside a small sprig for garnish. Remove the remaining mint leaves, wash and chop them, and add them to the blender along with the apple juice concentrate and orange juice. Blend thoroughly for 15 seconds.

Add the protein powder and milk and blend for 10 seconds.

Put ice cubes in a tall glass and pour the blender contents over the top. Thread the melon balls on to a cocktail skewer and lay it across the rim of the glass with the melon wedge. Garnish with the reserved mint sprig. Serve with a straw and a spoon.

Serves 1:

200 g (7 oz) watermelon (or honeydew or Galia melon)
2 sprigs fresh mint
1 tbsp apple juice concentrate
2 tbsp orange juice
2 tbsp protein powder
150 ml (5 fl oz) cold low-fat milk

Melons

Everyone knows that, with only 12 calories per 100 g (4 oz), melons are the ideal slimming fruit. But what many people don't know is that US cancer experts recommend melons because they contain large amounts of carotenoids. Melons support your kidneys, help prevent gout and rheumatism, and keep your blood thin. Researchers have found that melons contain adenosine, a chemical that acts like aspirin to prevent the clumping of blood platelets.

Apricot and Almond Shake

The beauty shake

Wash the apricots, cut them in half, and remove the stones. Set aside a nice apricot wedge for garnish. Chop the remaining fruit coarsely and put it in a blender, along with the apple juice concentrate, almond butter, and half of the milk. Blend for 15 seconds.

Serves 1:
2 or 3 fresh apricots (about 75 g (3 oz))
1 tbsp apple juice concentrate
2 tsp almond butter (from healtlhfood shop)
150 ml (5 fl oz) cold low-fat milk
2 tbsp protein powder
1 tsp vanilla extract
1–2 tbsp ground almonds

Add the remaining milk, protein powder, and vanilla extract. Blend briefly and vigorously.

Moisten the rim of a large glass with water, turn the glass upside-down, and dip the rim into the ground almonds.

Put ice cubes in the glass and pour the apricot mixture over the top. Cut part-way into the reserved apricot wedge and place it on the rim of the glass. Serve the drink with a fat straw.

Apricots

The Hunzas, a people in the Himalaya, live long lives. This could be because they eat so many apricots, a fruit with an especially high carotenoid content. Carotenoids are a plant pigment that render free radicals harmless, thus protecting your blood vessels, heart, and brain. Apricots also contain the beauty vitamin pantothenic acid, give you vitality, and boost fat degradation. Apricots' silicic acid strengthens connective tissue, meaning that it firms up your skin. They also provide large amounts of potassium, a natural diuretic.

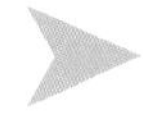

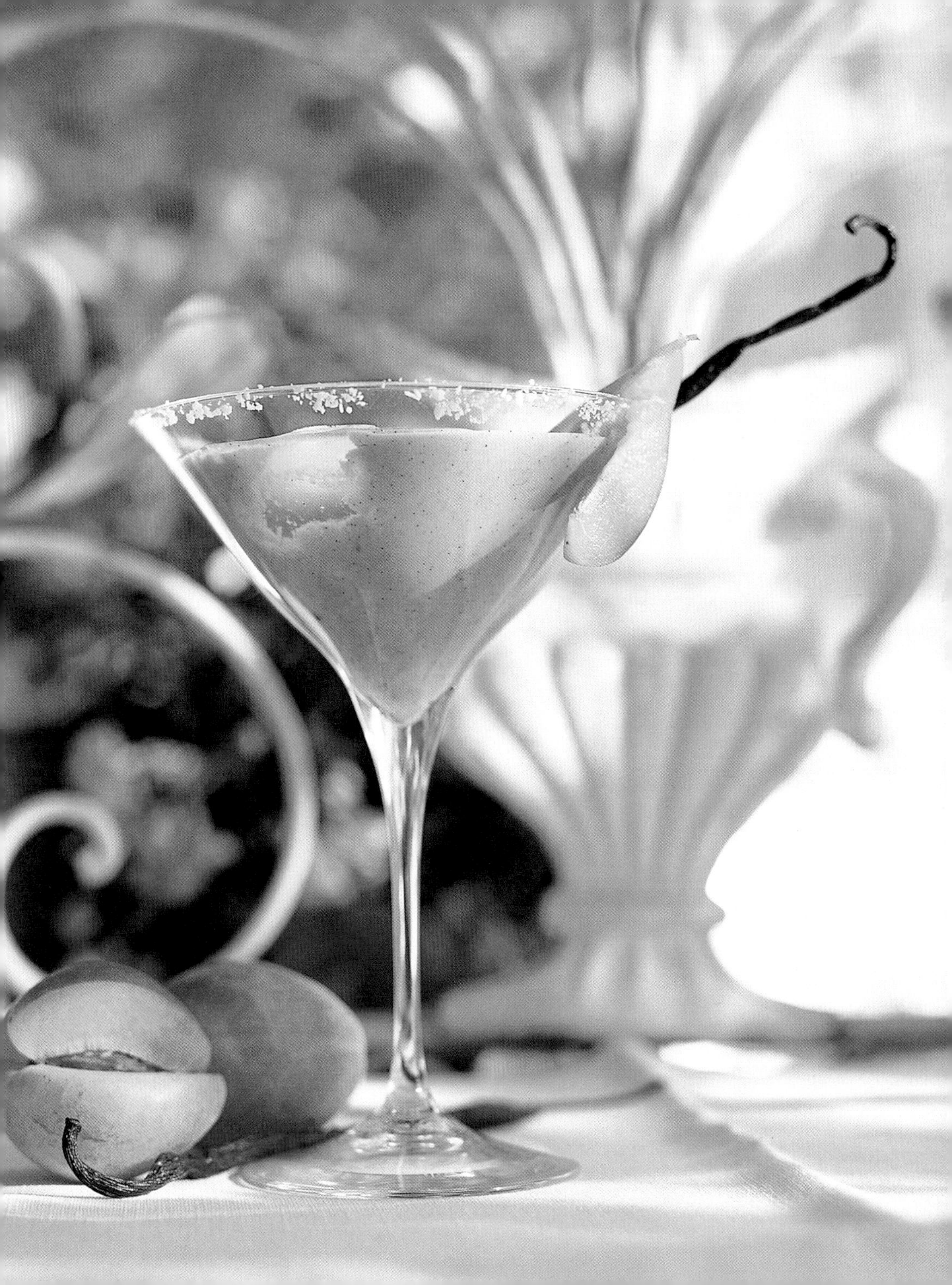

Citrus Buttermilk Flip

Sweet and sour shake

Cut a slice from each of the orange and lemon and set them aside for garnish. Peel the remaining orange. Remove the individual orange segments from their membranes, collecting the dripping juice. Place the orange segments and juice in a blender. Add the grapefruit juice, 1 tablespoon of the lemon juice, the egg yolk (if using), fructose, and half of the buttermilk. Blend the contents vigorously for 15 seconds.

Serves 1:

1 orange
1 lemon
2 tbsp freshly squeezed pink grapefruit juice
1 egg yolk (optional)
1 tbsp liquid fructose (from healthfood shop)
100 ml (3 1/2 fl oz) cold buttermilk
2 tbsp protein powder

Add the protein powder, a little finely grated zest from the lemon, and the remaining buttermilk and blend thoroughly for 10 seconds more.

Pour the mixture into a large glass. Cut part-way into the reserved orange and lemon slices and place them on the rim of the glass. Serve the drink with a straw.

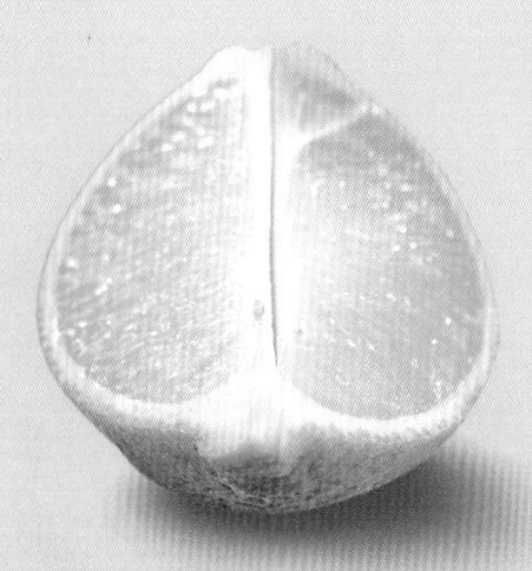

Citrus Fruits

We've all experienced the eye-opening effects of vitamin C in the morning, in the form of orange juice. But few of us are aware that the bioflavonoids in citrus fruits (especially in the pith) intensify the effects of the vitamin C. So don't peel your citrus fruits too carefully.

power

Chocolate and Pear Shake

Fruit for your sweet tooth

Heat the milk until lukewarm. Meanwhile, wash the pear, cut a wedge from it and set it aside for garnish. Peel the remaining pear, remove the core, cut the flesh into pieces, and put it in a blender. Add the orange juice, apple juice concentrate, chocolate (setting a little aside for garnish), and half of the milk. Blend thoroughly for 15 seconds.

Add the protein powder and the remaining milk and blend thoroughly for 10 seconds more.

Pour the mixture into a tall glass and place the pear wedge on the rim. Sprinkle the drink with the remaining chocolate and serve with a straw.

Serves 1:

150 ml (5 fl oz) low-fat milk
100 g (4 oz) ripe pear
1 tsp orange juice
1 tsp apple juice concentrate
2 tbsp finely grated unsweetened chocolate
2 tbsp protein powder

Chocolate

Chocolate doesn't have to make you fat. If it's unsweetened chocolate and contains more than 60 per cent cocoa, it doesn't affect insulin metabolism. Insulin, the fat-storing hormone, stays locked away so that glucagon, the fat-burning hormone, can break down the fat in the body. Interestingly cocoa beans supply more of the heart-protecting chemical polyphenol than a glass of red wine.

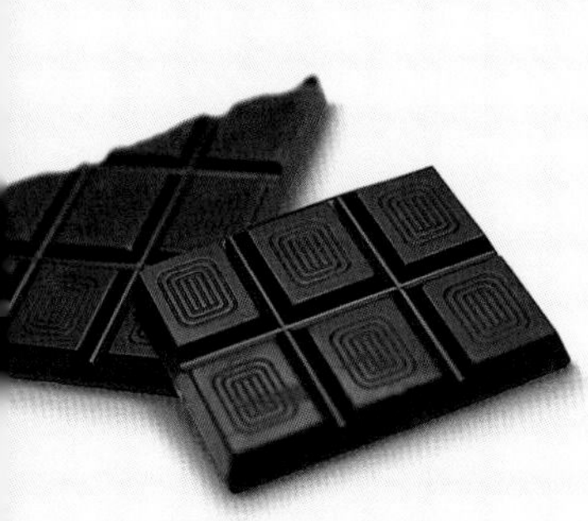

C-Packed Blueberry Shake

The drink of eternal youth

Rinse the fresh blueberries and pat dry, or thaw the frozen blueberries. Set aside ten nice berries for garnish. Place the remaining berries, lemon juice, and yogurt in a blender and blend thoroughly for 15 seconds.

Serves 1:
90 g (3 1/2 oz) blueberries (fresh or frozen)
1 tsp lemon juice
50 g (2 oz) probiotic yogurt (from healthfood shop)
2 tbsp protein powder
1 1/2 tsp ascorbic acid powder
100 ml (4 fl oz) cold low-fat milk

Add the protein powder, ascorbic acid powder, and milk and blend once more briefly and vigorously. Pour the mixture into a tall glass. Thread the reserved blueberries on to a cocktail skewer and lay it across the rim of the glass. Serve the drink with a fat straw.

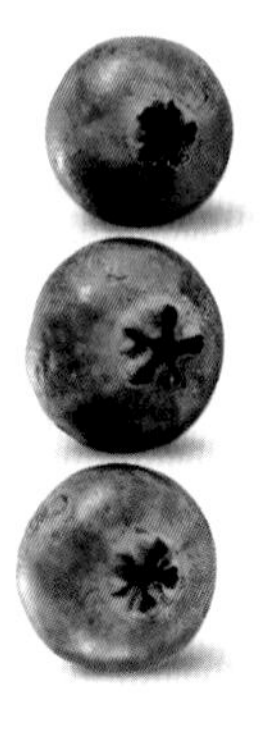

Blueberries

Blueberries are nature's lifestyle pills. They contain an entire pharmacy of bioactive ingredients. They help prevent cancer, fortify the immune system, lower cholesterol and blood fat levels, and relieve water retention. The tannins in blueberry skins strengthen your intestines and their anthocyanin (blue pigment) protects your cells, revitalizes your body, and keeps you young. Blueberries are the ideal accompaniment to probiotic yogurt, the drink of centenarians, supplemented by ascorbic acid powder, pure vitamin C.

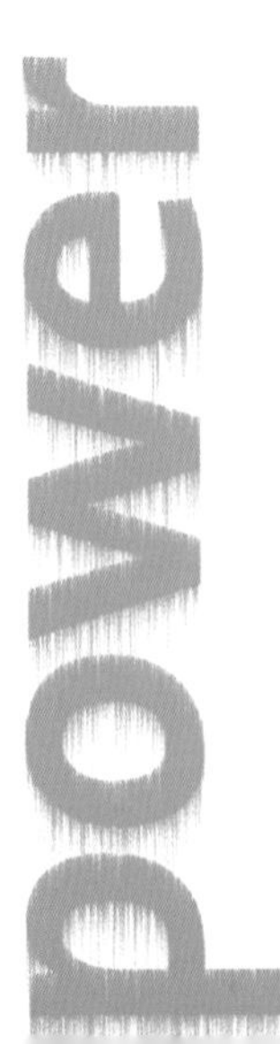

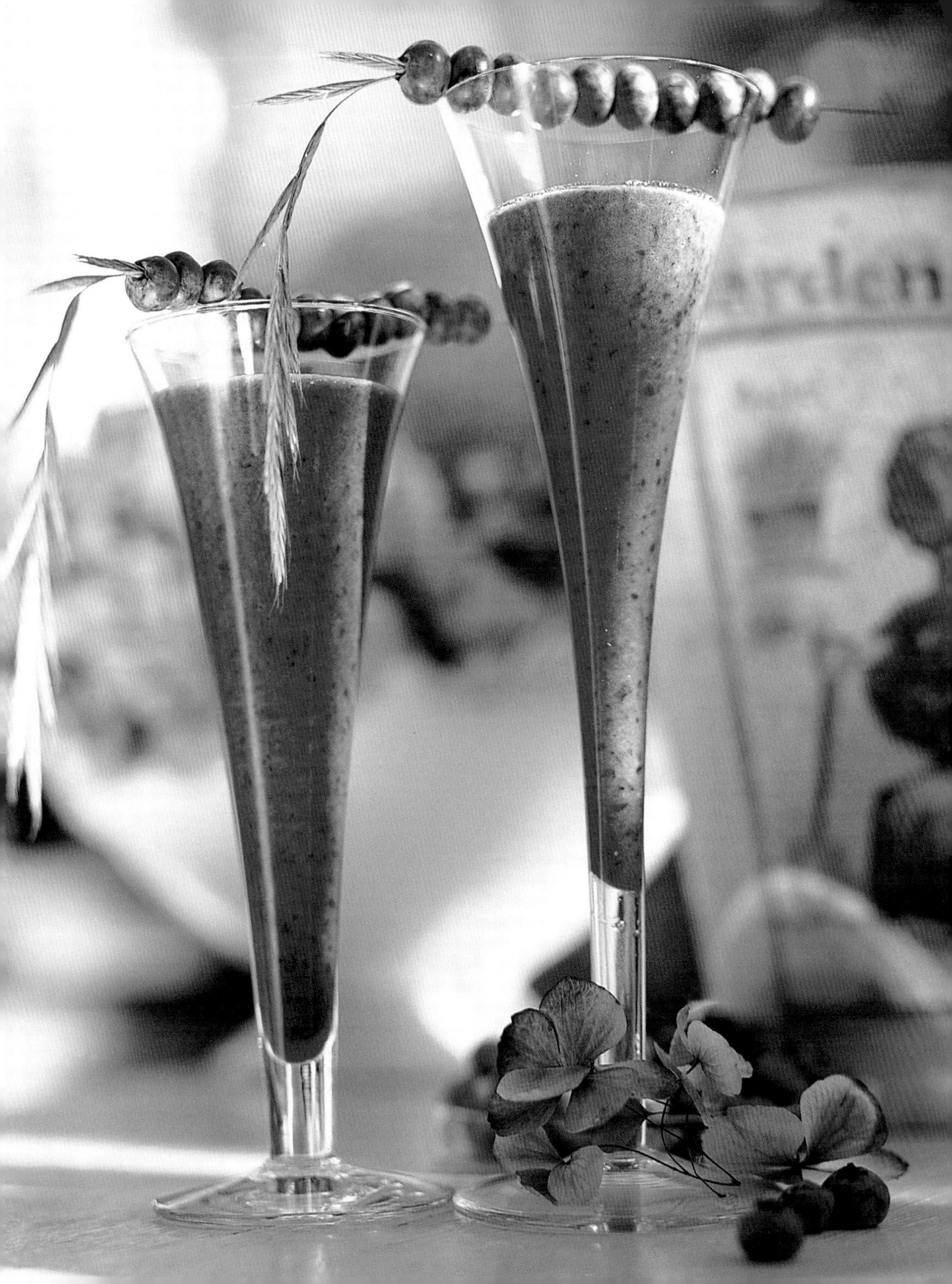

Cherry Buttermilk Drink

Purification cocktail

Wash the cherries and set aside a pair joined by their stems for garnish. Remove the stems and stones from the remaining cherries and put the cherries in a blender. Remove the leaves from the lemon balm and set aside one or two nice leaves. Chop the remaining lemon balm leaves and add them to the blender along with the lemon juice, apple juice concentrate, protein powder, and half of the buttermilk. Blend thoroughly for 15 seconds. Add the remaining buttermilk and blend for 10 seconds more. Pour the mixture into a tall glass, hang the reserved cherries over the rim of the glass, and garnish with the reserved mint leaves.

Serves 1:

100 g (4 oz) sweet cherries
1 sprig fresh lemon balm
1 tbsp lemon juice
2 tsp apple juice concentrate
2 tbsp protein powder
150 ml (5 fl oz) cold buttermilk

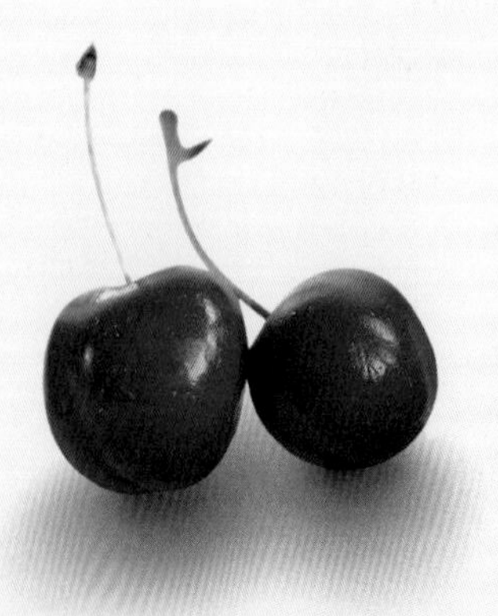

Cherries

Their minerals (potassium, iron, and calcium), vitamins (C and folic acid) and plant pigments (anthocyanin) purify, detoxify, boost connective tissue formation, stimulate blood production, prevent inflammation, and strengthen the immune system and bones. Cherry therapy rejuvenates you while it softens and cleanses your skin.

Apple and Nut Shake

For truly happy hours

Toss 2 tablespoons of the grated hazelnuts in an ungreased skillet over a medium heat until they smell toasted. Wash the apple half and set aside a nice wedge for garnish. Peel and core the remaining apple, chop the flesh, and put it in a blender. Add the lemon juice, cream, apple juice concentrate, and half of the milk and blend thoroughly for 15 seconds.

Add the toasted hazelnuts, protein powder, and the remaining milk and blend for 10 seconds more.

Brush a thin coating of honey on to the rim of a large glass and dip the glass into the remaining hazelnuts. Put ice cubes in the glass and pour in the apple and nut mixture. Serve with a straw.

Serves 1:

3 tbsp finely grated hazelnuts
100 g (4 oz) tart apple
1 tsp lemon juice
2 tbsp cream
1 tbsp apple juice concentrate
150 ml (5 fl oz) cold low-fat milk
2 tbsp protein powder
Honey

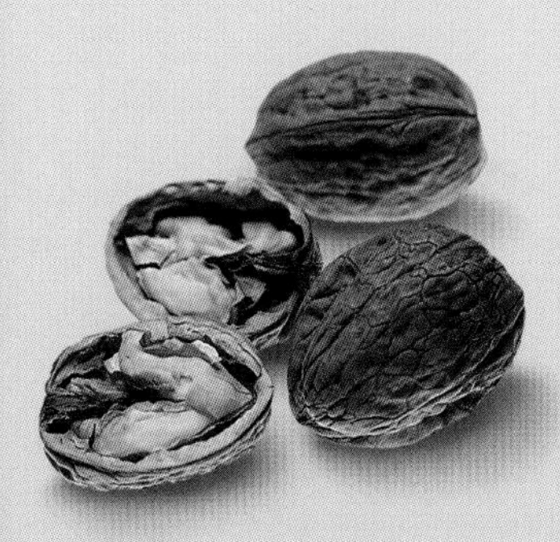

Nuts

Studies worldwide show that combining simple unsaturated fatty acids with the vitamin E in nuts protects your heart and circulation and slows down the ageing of your cells, especially your brain cells. Also, munching nuts raises your spirits, because nuts supply tryptophan, the material from which your body produces the youth hormone melatonin and the happy hormone serotonin. Nuts provide many minerals and salicylic acids, which prevent the clumping of blood platelets and thus help to prevent strokes.

power

Fit-for-fun cocktail

Banana and Yogurt Drink

Peel the banana and set aside two slices for garnish. Coarsely chop the remaining banana and place it in a blender. Add the lemon juice, honey, yogurt, and half of the milk. Blend for 15 seconds.

Serves 1:
1 large, ripe banana (about 100 g (4 oz))
1 tsp lemon juice
1 tbsp floral honey
50 g (2 oz) natural low-fat yogurt
100 ml (3 1/2 fl oz) cold low-fat milk
2 tbsp protein powder
1 lemon slice

Add the protein powder and the remaining milk and blend vigorously for 10 seconds more.

Pour the drink into a tall glass. Thread the lemon slice and banana slices on to a cocktail skewer and place inside the glass. Serve the drink with a straw.

Bananas

Bananas make you merry. Just 100 g (4 oz) supply 1.7 g of serotonin. This important neurotransmitter makes you serene and resistant to stress and puts you in a good mood. Bananas are a good fruit for people who lead high-stress lives because they soothe gastric complaints and fortify mucous membranes. Eat something green before the banana's valuable starch has been broken down into fructose and glucose, to help process its nutrients.

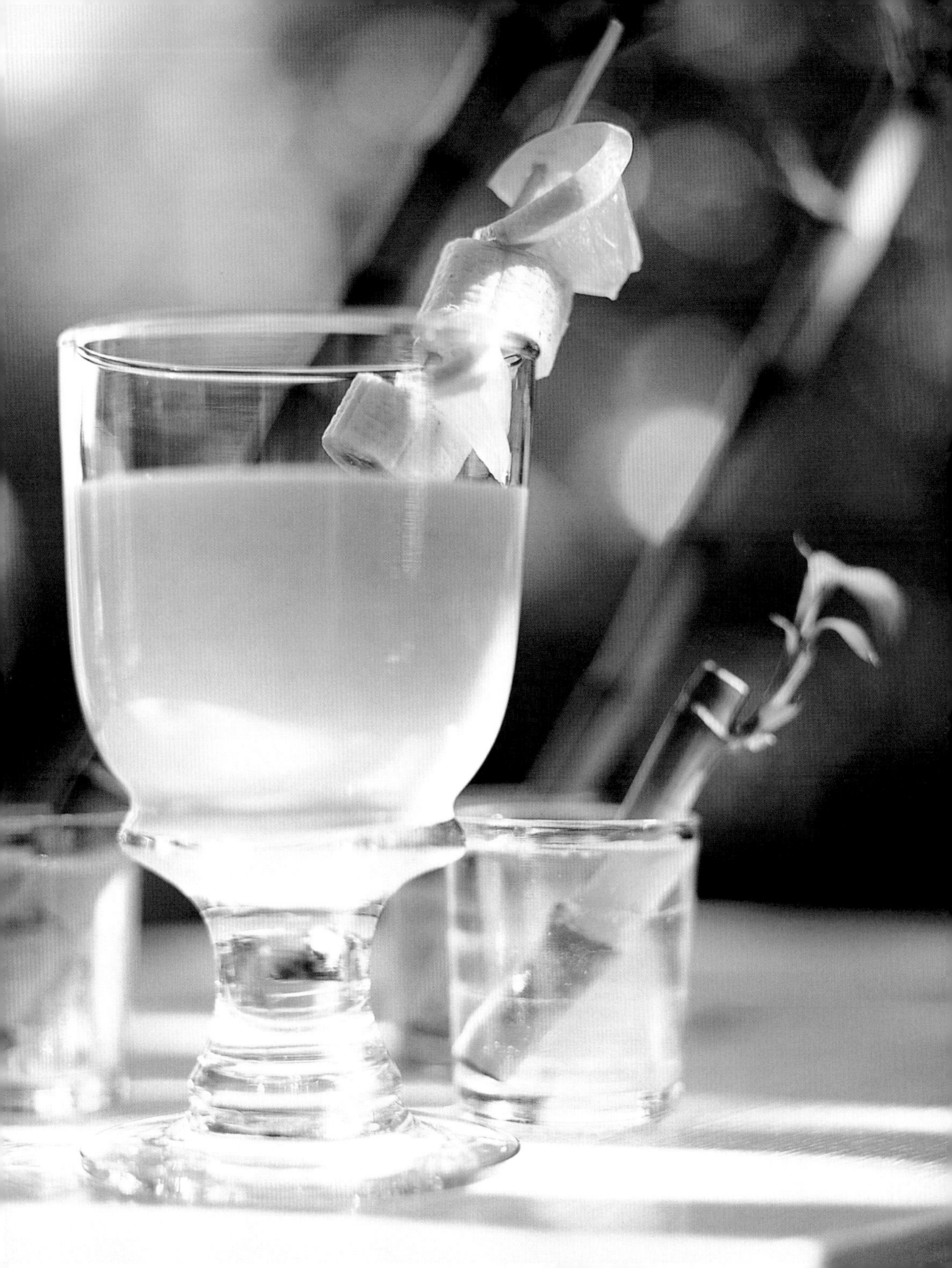

Berry Cherry Shake

Steadies the nerves

Wash and sort the blackberries. Set aside one blackberry for garnish. Put the remaining berries, apple juice concentrate, lemon juice, and cherry juice in a blender and blend thoroughly for 15 seconds. Rub the fruit mixture through a fine sieve to remove the seeds.

Pour the fruit mixture back into the blender, add the protein powder and cottage cheese, and blend vigorously for 10 seconds more.

Put ice cubes in a large glass, pour the mixture over the top, and garnish with whipped cream. Place the reserved blackberry on top. Serve the drink with a fat straw.

Serves 1:
80 g (3 oz) blackberries
2 tsp apple juice concentrate
1 tsp lemon juice
50 ml (2 fl oz) sour cherry juice (from healthfood shop)
2 tbsp protein powder
50 g (2 oz) cottage cheese
2 tbsp whipped cream

Blackberries

Blackberries supply loads of bioflavonoids – vitamins and minerals that keep you young, fortify your immune system, and arm your nerves against stress. These sweet, black, natural treasure chests contain carotenes, bioflavonoids, vitamin C, magnesium, and manganese.

power

Pineapple and Yogurt Drink

Lust for light

Remove the peel from the pineapple slice and set aside one piece of pineapple for garnish. Cut the remaining pineapple into small pieces, avoiding the core, and put the fruit in a blender.
Squeeze the juice from the grapefruit and add the juice to the blender along with the sugar. Blend thoroughly.
Add the yogurt and protein powder and blend at the lowest speed.
Put ice cubes in a tall glass and pour in the drink. Cut part-way into the pineapple piece and place it on the rim of the glass. Serve the drink with a fat straw.

Serves 1:
1 thick slice of fresh pineapple (about 100 g (4 oz) with peel)
1/2 yellow grapefruit
2 tsp brown sugar
100 g (4 oz) probiotic yogurt (from healthfood shop)
2 tbsp protein powder

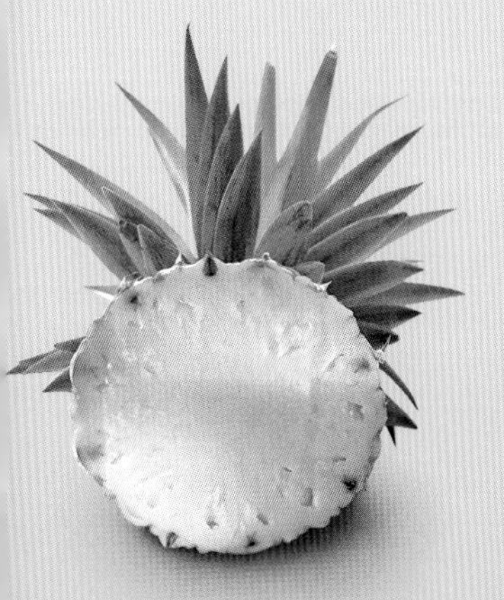

Pineapple

This exquisite tropical fruit is bursting with potassium, magnesium, phosphorus, iron, copper, zinc, manganese and iodine, all minerals that promote fat metabolism. The main contribution of pineapple to fitness is the enzyme bromelain, which aids in the digestion of protein. It guarantees that the important amino acids arrive at their place of effectiveness, your cells.
Weight-loss tip: Eat a slice of fresh pineapple before every meal.

power

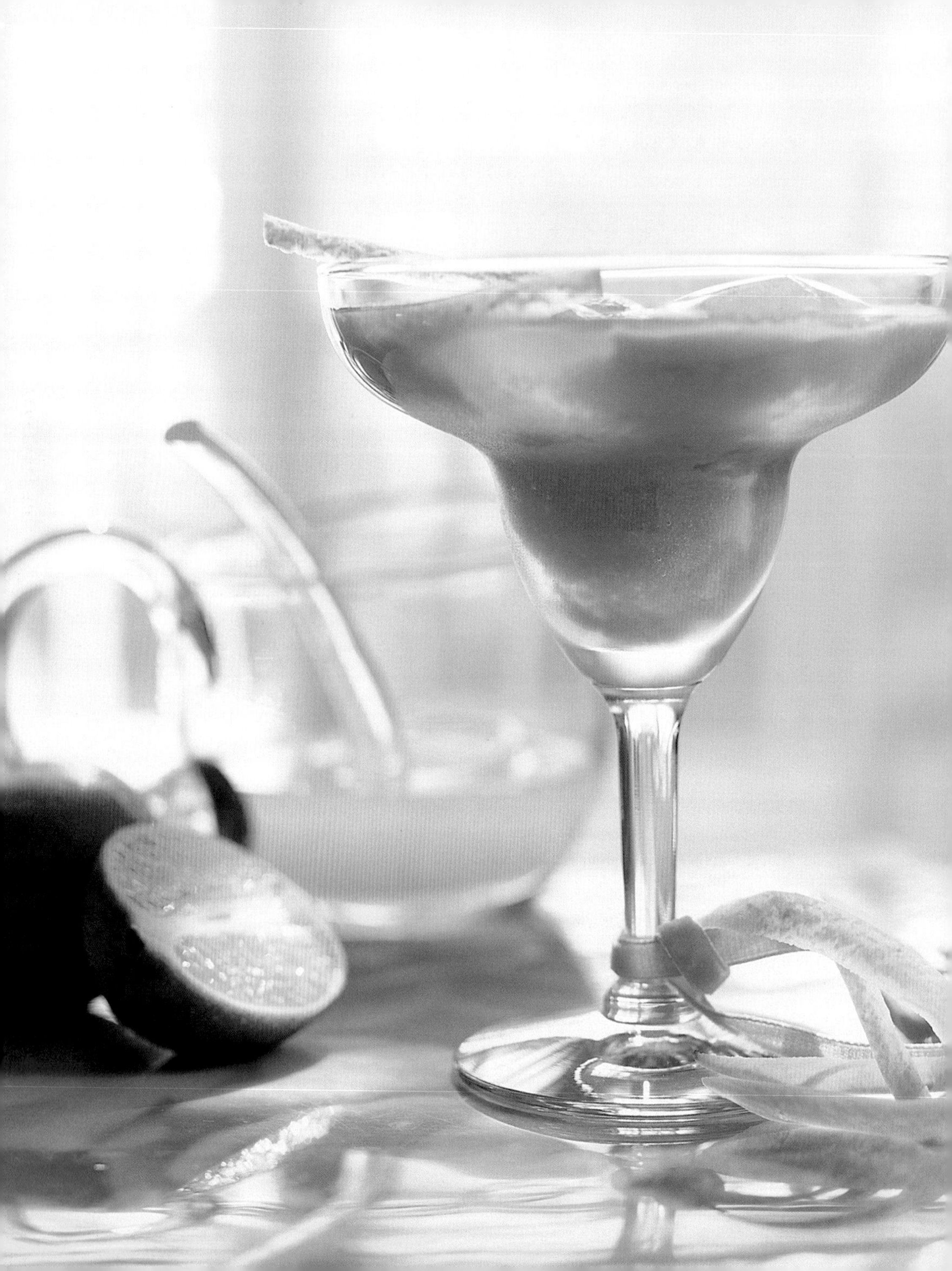

Mango and Carrot Mix

The drink of eternal youth, take two

Peel the mango. Cut a mango wedge and set it aside for garnish. Coarsely chop the remaining mango and put it in a blender. Add the lime juice, honey, and half of the carrot juice and blend for 15 seconds.

Add the remaining carrot juice, protein powder, and ginger and blend well for 10 seconds more.

Put ice cubes in a large glass and pour the mixture over the top. Place the mango wedge and carrot strips on the rim of the glass. Serve the drink with a straw.

Serves 1:

100 g (4 oz) mango
1 tbsp lime juice
2 tsp floral honey
150 ml (5 fl oz) cold carrot juice
2 tbsp protein powder
2 pinches ground ginger
2 carrot strips (use a vegetable peeler)

Mangoes

This fruit seduces you with its unique flavour and incomparable provitamin A content. With 6000 I.U. of vitamin A, mangoes beat every other fruit and any vitamin pill. Only carrots can keep up – and the two together are an ideal combination. Anti-ageing vitamin A prevents cancer and blocks free radicals, the destructive substances that cause your cells to age faster. Take care: don't drink milk or alcohol two hours before or after eating mangoes, to avoid upsetting your stomach.

power

Tomato and Avocado Drink

A spicy revitalizer

Peel the avocado, dice the flesh, and put it in a blender. Drizzle with the lemon juice. Add half of the tomato juice and blend thoroughly for 15 seconds.

Serves 1:
40 g (1 1/2 oz) ripe avocado
2 tbsp lemon juice
100 ml (3 1/2 fl oz) cold tomato juice
2 tbsp protein powder
50 ml (2 fl oz) mineral water
Salt to taste
Pepper to taste
Several drops of Tabasco sauce
2 cherry tomatoes

Add the protein powder, the remaining tomato juice, and the mineral water. Season to taste with salt, pepper, and Tabasco. Blend vigorously for 10 seconds. Put ice cubes in a glass and pour the mixture over the top. Wash the cherrry tomatoes, pat them dry, and use them to garnish the drink. Serve the drink with a straw.

Tomatoes

Doctors prescribe these "love apples" as an anti-cancer food (due to the lycopene), as a tonic for your heart and kidneys, and as a remedy for gout and rheumatism. Tomatoes are low in calories and their potassium content makes them a diuretic. They're rich in magnesium, calcium, iron, and zinc. Tomatoes' nutrients stimulate digestion, clean out your intestines, and keep you slim. And tomatoes improve your mood. A tomato drink in the morning makes you feel alive and optimistic and helps you deal with stress.

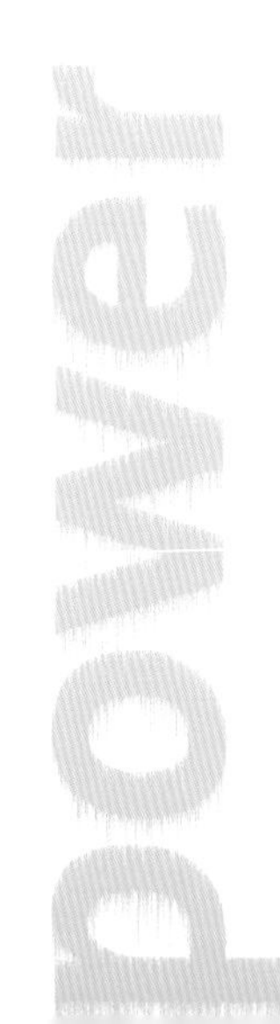

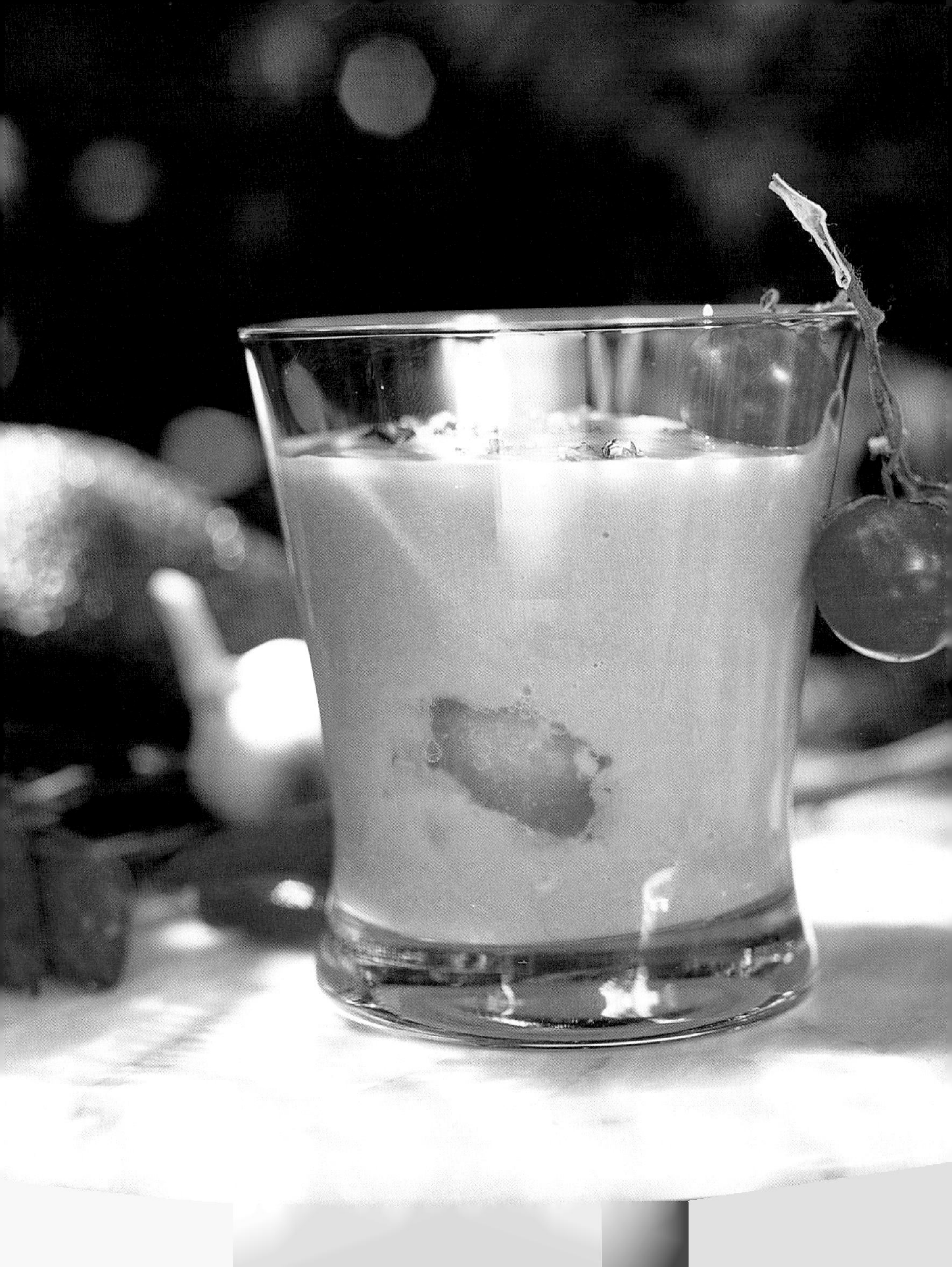

Spicy Vegetable Shake

Good mood mix

Wash and trim the red pepper and tomatoes. Peel the celeriac. Set aside a couple of pieces of red pepper and a cherry tomato for garnish. Dice the remaining vegetables. Rinse the parsley, set aside a small sprig for garnish, remove the remaining leaves from the stalks, and chop the leaves coarsely. Put the red pepper, celeriac, tomatoes, and parsley in a blender. Add the tomato juice and blend thoroughly for 15 seconds. Add the protein powder and stock, and season with herb salt and pepper. Blend vigorously for 10 seconds more. Pour the drink into a tall glass. Thread the reserved pieces of red pepper and the cherry tomato on to a cocktail skewer and lay it across the rim of the glass. Garnish with the reserved parsley.

Serves 1:

50 g (2 oz) red pepper
2–3 cherry tomatoes
50 g (2 oz) celeriac
3 sprigs fresh Italian parsley
100 ml (3 1/2 fl oz) cold tomato juice
2 tbsp protein powder
75 ml (3 fl oz) vegetable stock
Herb salt to taste
Black pepper to taste

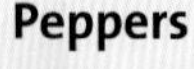

Peppers

Peppers are pure tonic. Their capsicin and vitamin C fortify your immune system and their carotene (especially in red peppers) prevents cancer. Peppers aid digestion and circulation, work as a diuretic, ease pain, reduce stress, firm up connective tissue, improve concentration, and combat arthritis.

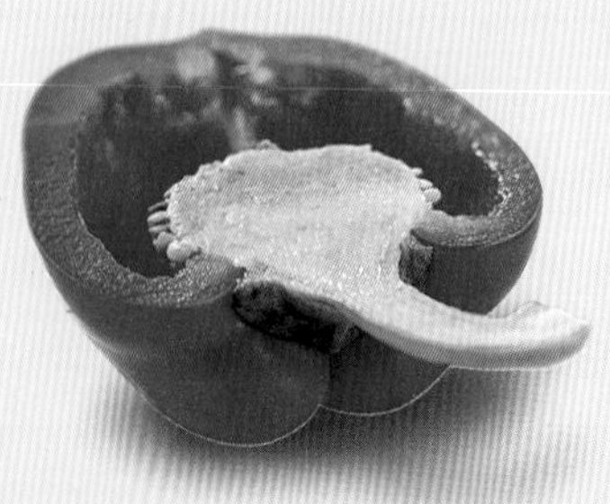

power

Icy Cucumber Dill Drink

The fit and trim drink

Dice the frozen cucumber and put it in a blender. Rinse the dill and set aside a sprig for garnish. Remove the remaining leaves from the stalks, chop the leaves coarsely, and add them to the blender along with the lemon juice, and half the yogurt. Blend thoroughly for 15 seconds.

Add the protein powder and the remaining yogurt. Season with salt and pepper and blend thoroughly for 10 seconds more.

Put ice cubes in a wide glass and pour the mixture over the top.

Cut part-way into the reserved cucumber slice and place it on the rim of the glass with the reserved dill. Serve the drink with a straw.

Serves 1:

75 g (3 oz) frozen cucumber (without peel or seeds)
3 small sprigs fresh dill
1 tsp lemon juice
150 ml (5 fl oz) probiotic yogurt (from healthfood shop)
2 tbsp protein powder
Salt to taste
Black pepper to taste
1 slice cucumber

Cucumbers

With only thirteen calories per 100 g (4 oz) and an insulin-like hormone, cucumbers are true fat burners. For their magnesium and potassium, cucumbers have been dubbed the fruit of athletes. Their juice drives water out of your body, making it easier on your heart. Cucumbers' bitter constituents stimulate the liver and gall bladder. Doctors prescribe cucumbers for gout and rheumatism as well as for cleansing the skin. A slice of cucumber on your skin can smooth wrinkles, soothe minor rashes, and relieve eczema.

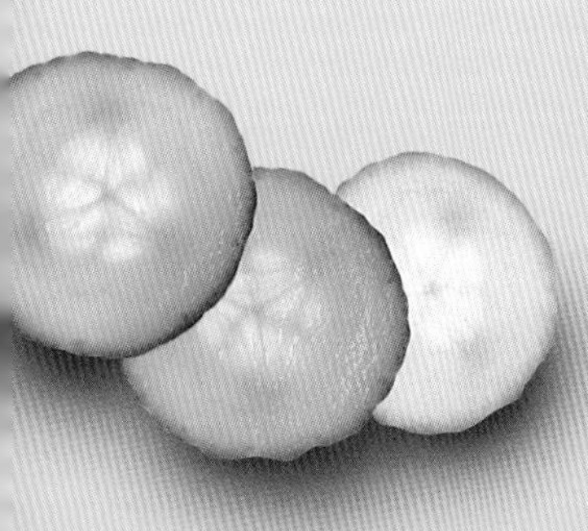

power

Green temptation

Carrot and Herb Shake

Wash the herbs and shake them dry. Set aside a small sprig of chervil for garnish. Remove the remaining chervil and parsley leaves from their stalks and chop the leaves finely. Put the herbs in a blender along with the lemon juice, honey, hazelnuts, and carrot juice. Blend vigorously for 15 seconds.

Add the protein powder and milk. Season with salt, pepper, Worcestershire sauce, and olive oil. Blend for 10 seconds more.

Pour the drink into a tall glass. Lay the carrot stick across the rim of the glass and garnish the drink with the reserved chervil.

Serves 1:

1 handful fresh chervil
3 sprigs fresh Italian parsley
1 tbsp lemon juice
1 tsp floral honey
2 tbsp ground hazelnuts
75 ml (3 fl oz) cold carrot juice
2 tbsp protein powder
100 ml (3 1/2 fl oz) cold low-fat milk
Salt to taste
Black pepper to taste
1–2 drops Worcestershire sauce
2 drops olive oil
1 carrot stick

Carrots

Due to their high pectin content (a fibre that promotes healthy intestines) and skin-protecting vitamin A, carrots are an essential ingredient in fitness cocktails. Tip: always consume them with a little olive oil so that their vitamin A can be transported easily to your cells.

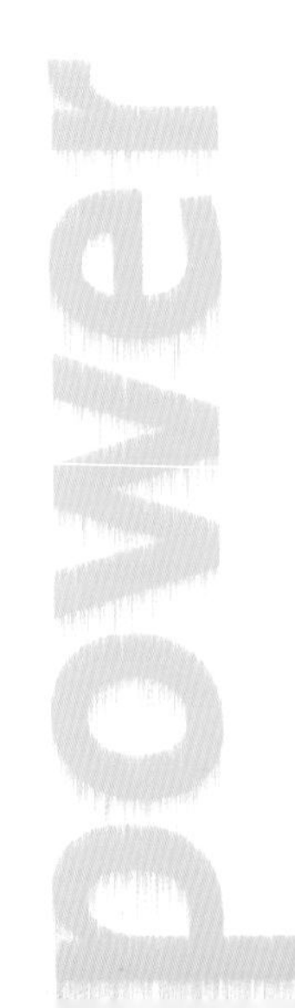

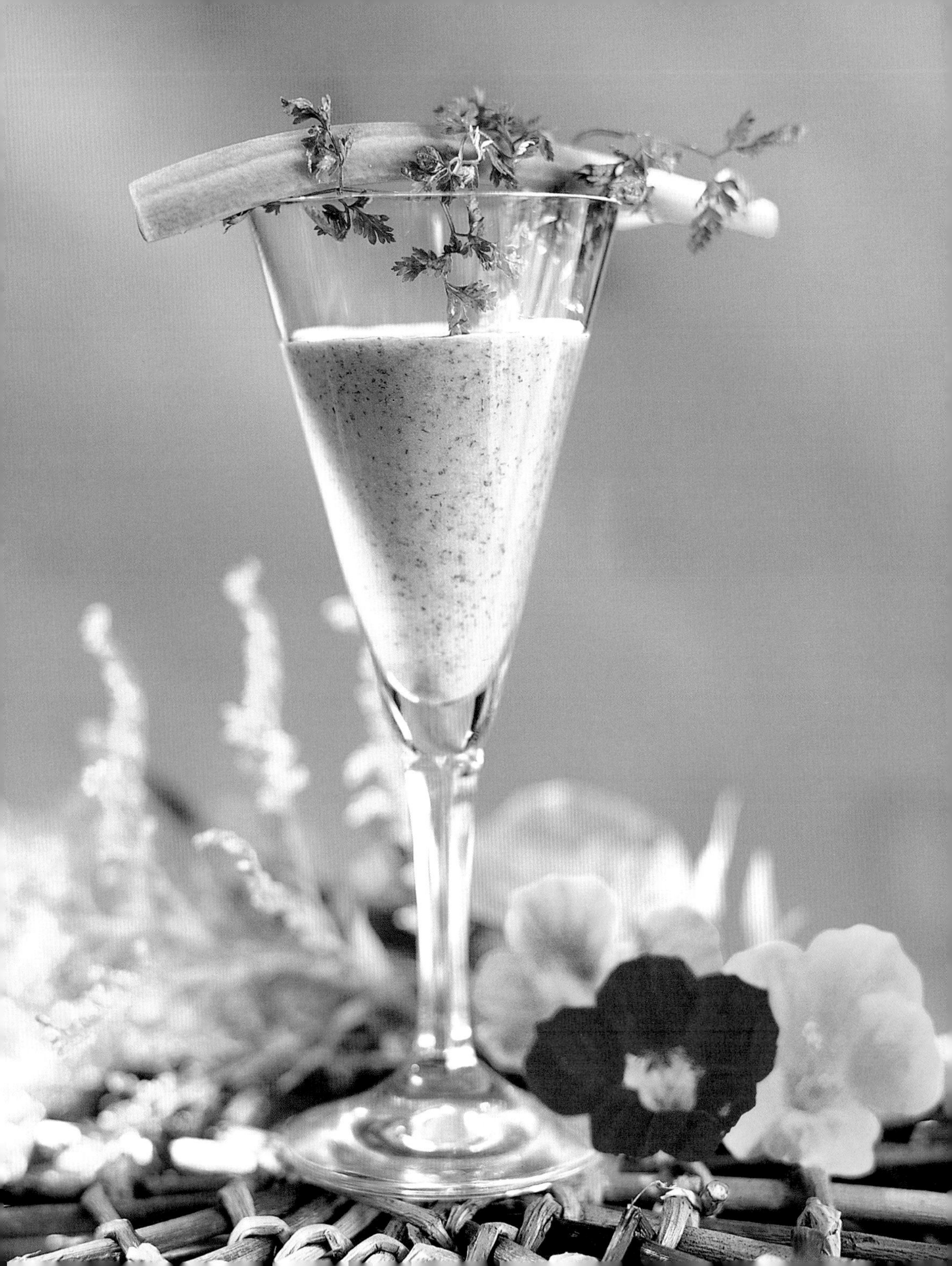

Beetroot Cream

For a long life

Wash and trim the radishes. Cut two slices from the radishes and set them aside for garnish. Chop the remaining radishes and put them in a blender along with the yogurt, beetroot juice, lemon juice, and horseradish. Blend well for 15 seconds.

Add the protein powder and buttermilk. Season generously with salt and pepper and blend thoroughly for 10 seconds more. Pour the mixture into a large glass. Cut part-way into the radish slices and place them on the rim of the glass. Sprinkle with the chives. Serve the drink with a fat straw.

Serves 1:

4–5 radishes (50 g (2 oz))
2 tbsp low-fat natural yogurt
50 ml (2 fl oz) beetroot juice
2 tsp lemon juice
1/2 tsp grated horseradish
2 tbsp protein powder
125 ml (4 fl oz) cold buttermilk
Salt to taste
Black pepper to taste
1 tsp chopped fresh chives

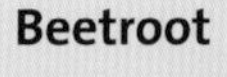

Beetroot

These anti-ageing vegetables provide two fountains of youth: folic acid and silicium. Folic acid protects blood vessels and the heart and is involved in the production of hormones such as dopamine and norepinephrine that promote good moods, creativity, and power. Silicium is the trace element for beauty. It fortifies connective tissue and gives you firm skin, shiny hair, and hard nails. Beetroot also detoxifies your body, works as a diuretic, and promotes cell growth and the formation of red blood cells.

power

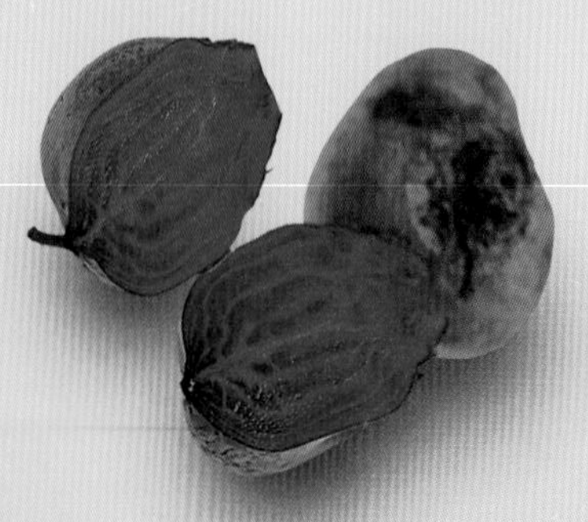

Celeriac and Spinach Flip

The anti-stress shake

Peel the celeriac, set aside a narrow wedge for garnish and grate the remainder. Wash the spinach thoroughly, trim it, and chop it coarsely. Rinse the parsley and set aside a small sprig for garnish. Remove the remaining parsley leaves from the stalks and chop the leaves.

Put the celeriac, spinach, and parsley in a blender. Add the egg yolk (if using), lemon juice, and celeriac juice. Blend well for 15 seconds. Add the protein powder and milk. Season with salt, pepper, and nutmeg and blend thoroughly for 10 seconds more. Pour the mixture into a tall glass. Cut part-way into the celeriac wedge and place it on the rim of the glass. Grind a little pepper over the top and garnish with the reserved parsley. Serve the drink with a straw.

Serves 1:

50 g (2 oz) celeriac
40 g (1 1/2 oz) tender spinach leaves
3 sprigs fresh Italian parsley
1 egg yolk (optional)
2 tsp lemon juice
50 ml (2 fl oz) celeriac juice (from healthfood shop)
2 tbsp protein powder
100 ml (4 fl oz) cold low-fat milk
Salt to taste
Black pepper to taste
1 pinch freshly ground nutmeg

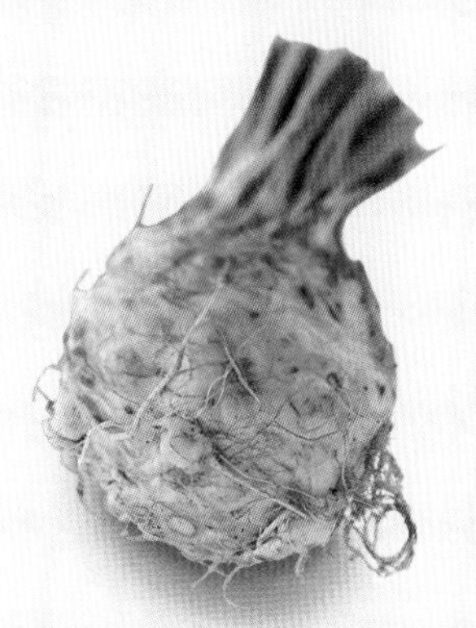

Celeriac

This vegetable lowers stress-related high blood pressure. In Asia, celeriac has been used for 2000 years as a blood pressure-reducing remedy. The active substance 3-N-butyl phthalide reduces the stress hormones in the blood that constrict blood vessels. Certainly Hippocrates wasn't aware of this, but he still recommended celeriac for everyone "whose nerves flutter".

power

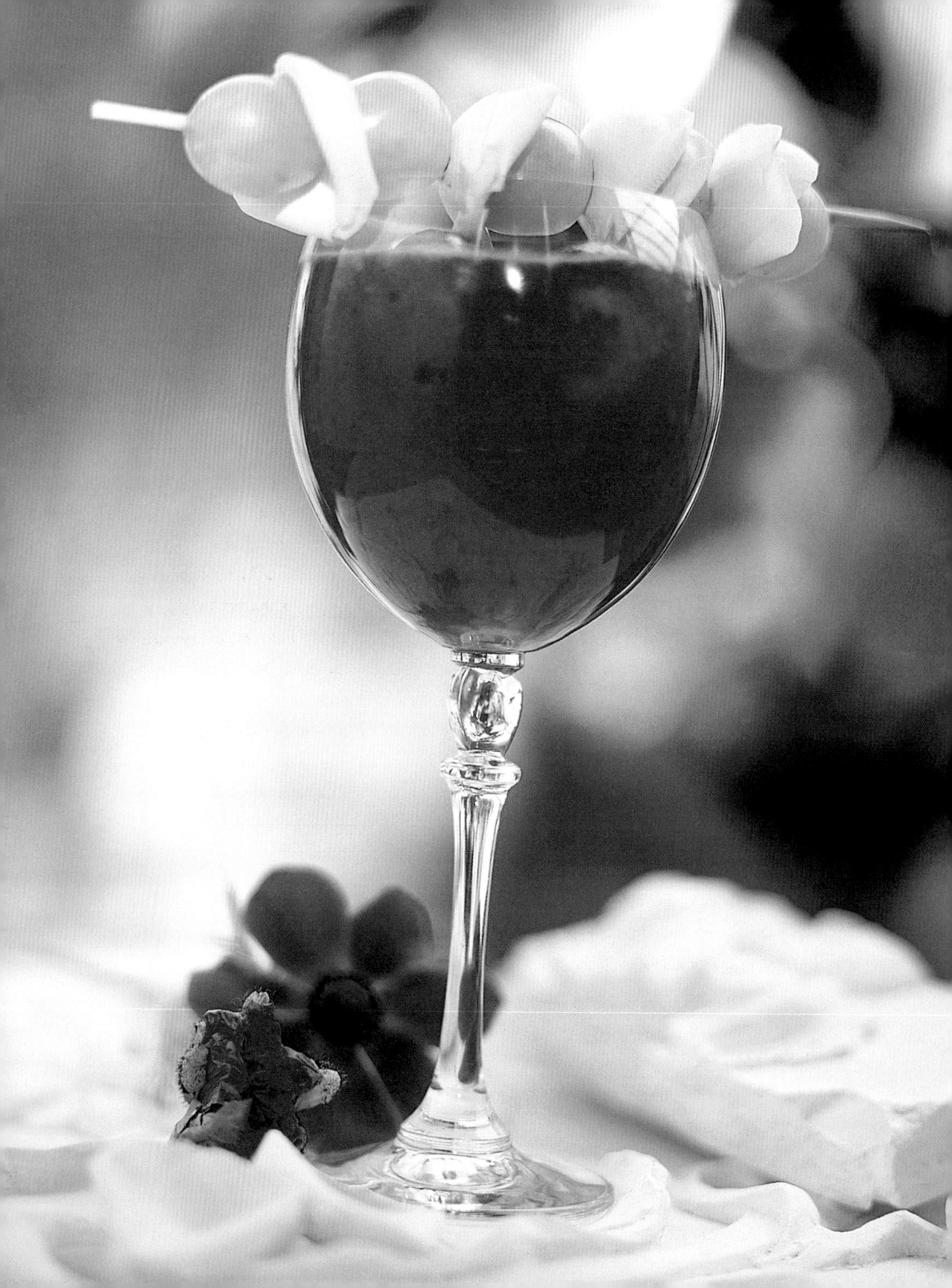

Tutti-frutti Cocktail

Nature's energy drink

Wash and trim or peel the fruit. Set aside several pieces for garnish. Cut the remaining fruit into small pieces and put them in a blender along with the lemon juice, fructose, cottage cheese, and half of the low-fat milk. Blend thoroughly for 15 seconds.

Add the protein powder, instant porridge flakes, and the remaining milk and blend well for 10 seconds. Put ice cubes in a large glass and pour the mixture over the top. Thread the reserved fruit on to a small cocktail skewer and lay it across the rim of the glass. Serve the drink with a fat straw.

Serves 1:

100 g (4 oz) mixed fruit, e.g. strawberries, green grapes, blackberries, bananas

2 tsp lemon juice

1 tbsp liquid fructose (from healthfood shop)

2 tbsp low-fat cottage cheese

125 ml (4 fl oz) cold low-fat milk

3 tbsp protein powder

2 tbsp instant porridge flakes

Grapes

Grapes contain boron, which strengthens bones and helps prevent osteoporosis. Their B vitamins steady your nerves, their folic acid stimulates blood production, their vitamin C feeds your immune system, their potassium lowers your blood pressure, and their magnesium fortifies your muscles and heart. Grapes keep your intestines and kidneys functioning and promote better concentration.

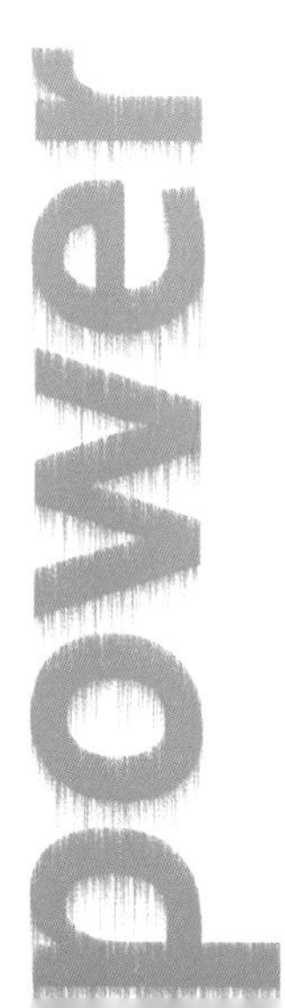

Mocha Banana Dream

With stimulating espresso

Put the espresso coffee and sugar in a blender. Peel the banana, cut it into several pieces, and add them to the blender along with half the milk.

Serves 1:
4 tbsp cold espresso coffee
1 tsp brown sugar
60 g (2 oz) banana
150 ml (5 fl oz) cold low-fat milk
3 tbsp protein powder
1 tbsp instant espresso powder
1 tbsp whipped cream

Blend thoroughly for 10 seconds.

Add the protein powder and the remaining milk and blend vigorously for 10 seconds more.

Moisten the rim of a tall glass and dip it into the espresso powder. Put ice cubes in a tall glass and pour the mixture over the top. Garnish with the whipped cream and the remaining espresso powder.

Serve the drink with a straw and a long-handled spoon.

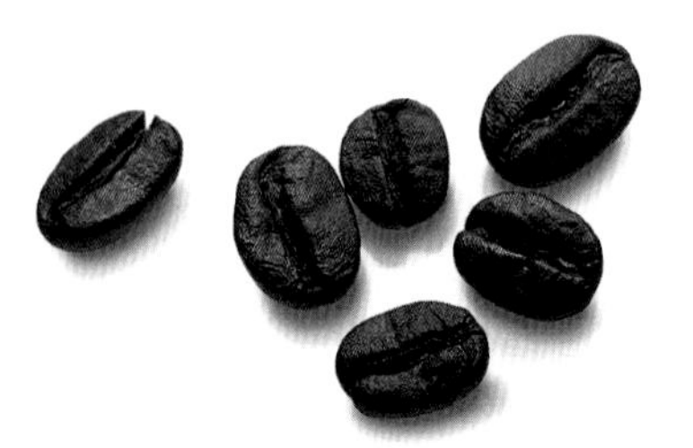

Coffee

The components of coffee boost the metabolism and stimulate brain activity. Coffee drinkers read faster, have a better short-term memory, and have a 40 per cent lower risk of gall stones than non-coffee drinkers. Caffeine not only expands minds but also expands constricted bronchial tubes (asthma). Researchers in Scotland found that heart disease is more common in people who don't drink coffee. A healthy dose: one to three cups per day.

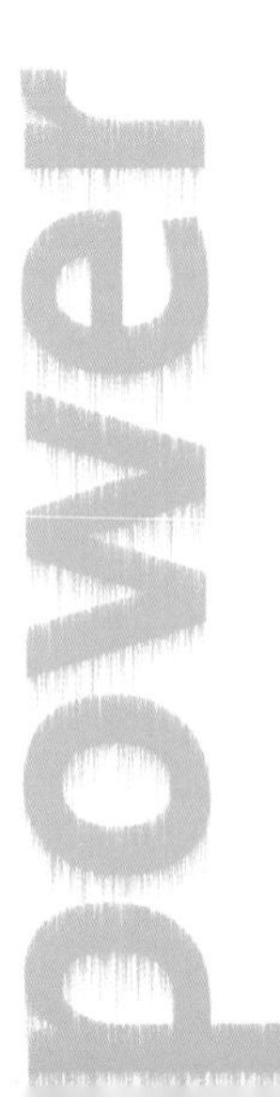

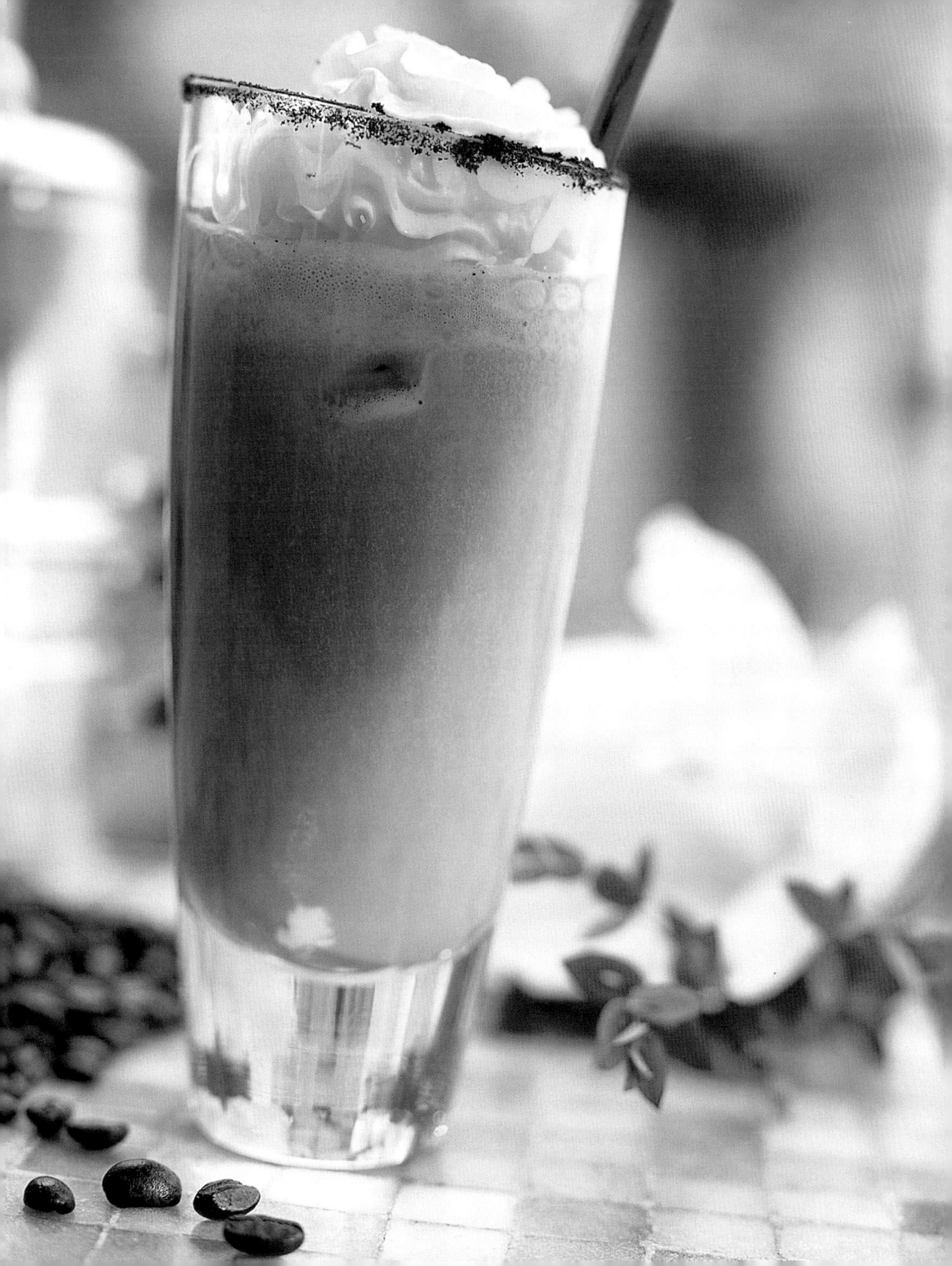

Chocolate Apricot Shake

Gives feelings of love

Gradually bring the milk to the boil. Chop the chocolate coarsely, add it to the milk, and melt it, stirring occasionally.

Serves 1:

200 ml (7 fl oz) low-fat milk
50 g (2 oz) unsweetened chocolate
1 tsp lemon juice
3 tbsp protein powder
1 tsp vanilla extract
1 scoop apricot sorbet
1/2 slice orange

Remove the chocolate milk from the heat, pour it into a heatproof jug, and refrigerate for 30 minutes. Pour the cooled chocolate milk into a blender. Add the lemon juice, protein powder, and vanilla extract and blend well for 15 seconds.

Put the arpicot sorbet in a tall glass and pour the chocolate milk over the top. Cut part-way into the orange slice and place it on the rim of the glass. Serve the drink with a long-handled spoon and a straw. Orange is a good alternative to apricot.

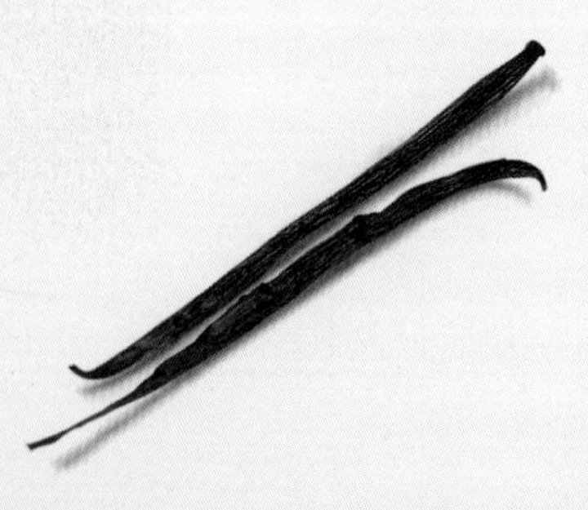

Vanilla

This black pod, whose pulp lends desserts an incomparable flavour, originated in Central America and is a member of the orchid family. Vanilla stimulates the kidneys, fortifies the stomach, and promotes good digestion. The wives of Aztec rulers knew the effects of cocoa drinks seasoned with vanilla on their men. Vanilla was once forbidden in monasteries.

power

Tangy Lime Shake

Sour power

Wash the lime in hot water, dry it, and cut a fine strip of the peel. Finely grate the rest of the zest. Cut the lime in half and squeeze the juice from both halves.

Put the lime juice, lime zest, cream cheese, and cream in a blender. Add the sugar and half the milk and blend for 15 seconds.

Add the protein powder and the remaining milk and blend thoroughly for 10 seconds more.

Pour the mixture into a large glass. Cut partway into the strawberry and place it on the rim of the glass. Garnish the drink with the strip of lime peel and serve it with a fat straw.

Serves 1:

1 lime (or 1/2 lemon)
75 g (3 oz) low-fat cream cheese
2 tbsp cream
2 tsp brown sugar
150 ml (5 fl oz) cold low-fat milk
3 tbsp protein powder
1 ripe firm strawberry

Lime

Although this "lemon of the tropics" has less vitamin C than its big sister the lemon, it provides other benefits. It is rich in potassium, calcium, phosphorous, and aromatic oils. And it cheers the organic heart because its rind is usually untreated, allowing you to grate it and use its healthy bitter constituents as a spice.

power

Raspberry and Poppy Seed Cream

Sweet, irresistible seduction

In a saucepan, bring the milk and cream to a boil. Slit open the vanilla pod lengthwise, scrape out the pulp and add the pod and pulp to the milk. Sprinkle in two-thirds of the poppy seeds and simmer for 5 minutes. Remove the vanilla pod.

Serves 1:

125 ml (4 fl oz) cold low-fat milk
2 tbsp cream
1/2 vanilla pod
1 tbsp poppy seeds
100 g (4 oz) raspberries
1 tbsp maple syrup
3 tsp lemon juice
3 tbsp protein powder
1 lemon slice

Rinse the raspberries and sort them. Set aside four nice berries for garnish. Put the remaining raspberries, maple syrup, 2 teaspoons of the lemon juice, and 6 tablespoons of the poppy seed and milk mixture in the blender and blend for 15 seconds. Add the protein powder and the remaining poppy seed and milk mixture and blend for 10 seconds more. Moisten the rim of a glass with the remaining lemon juice and dip it into the remaining poppy seeds. Pour the milk mixture into the glass. Thread the lemon slice and reserved raspberries on to a cocktail skewer and lay it across the rim of the glass. Serve the drink with a straw.

Raspberries

In France, raspberries are considered to be a medicinal plant. They spice up your health with potassium (to reduce blood pressure), iron (to promote blood production), and magnesium (to fortify heart and muscles). Their acids, pectin, and tannins aid the liver in detoxifying the body and even reduce fevers. Raspberries' biotin adds shine to your hair, their seeds stimulate digestion, and their carotenes protect your skin and sharpen your vision.

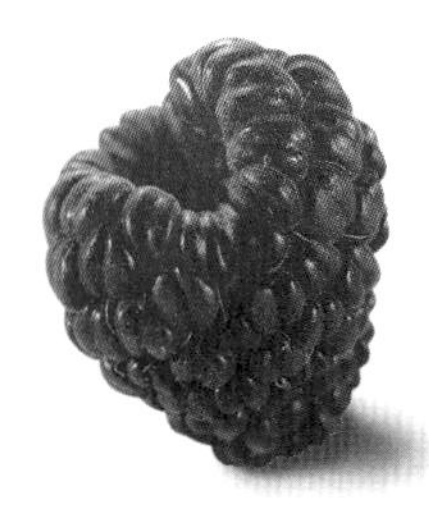

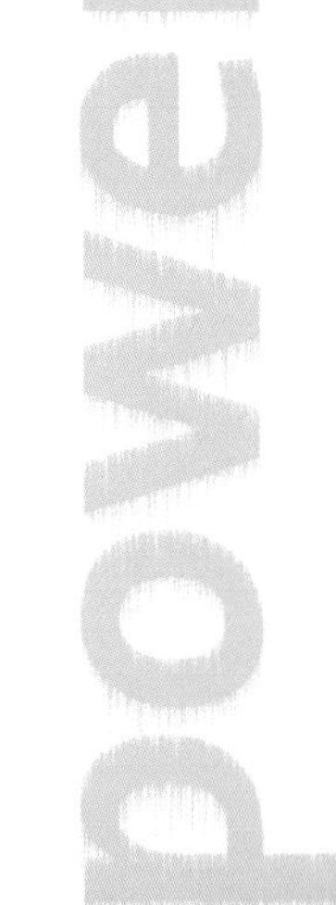

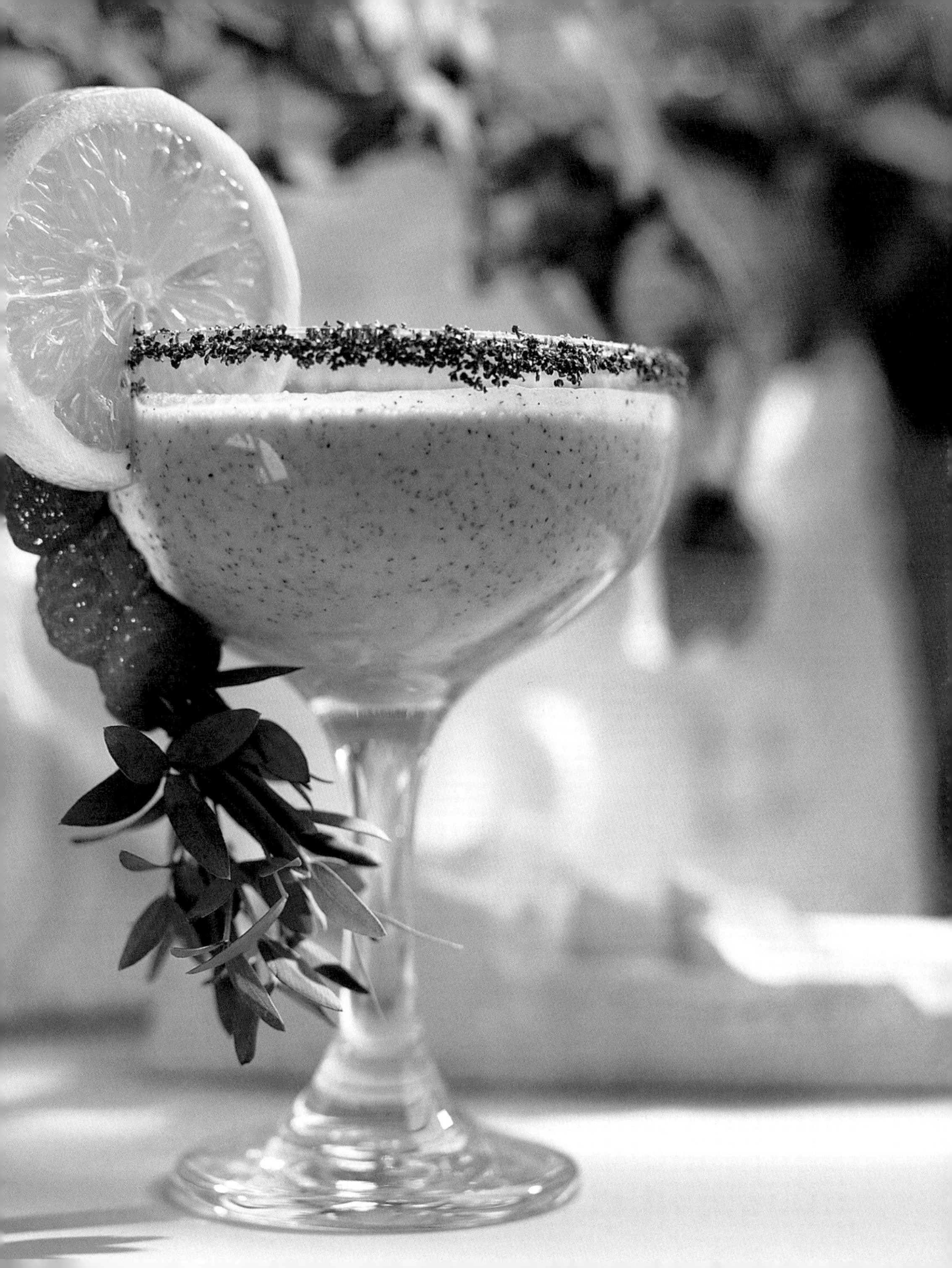

Index

A

Almond, apricot shake 30
Amino acids, about 4–5

Apple(s)
- about 23
- and elderberry drink 24
- and nut shake 37

Apricot(s)
- about 30
- and almond shake 30

Avocado(s)
- about 22
- kiwi, mix 22
- tomato, drink 44

B

Banana(s)
- about 38
- and yogurt drink 38
- blackcurrant and, shake 27
- mocha, dream 54

Beetroot
- about 50
- cream 50

Berry(ies)
- about 13
- -cherry shake 40
- smoothie 13

Blackberries, about 40

Blackcurrant(s)
- about 27
- and banana shake 27

Blueberry(ies)
- about 34
- C-packed, shake 34

Buttermilk
- and cherry drink 36
- citrus, flip 32

C

Carrot(s)
- about 48
- and herb shake 48
- mango, mix 43

Celeriac
- about 51
- and spinach flip 51

Citrus
- buttermilk flip 32
- fruits, about 32

Cherry(ies)
- about 36
- berry, shake 40
- buttermilk drink 36

Chocolate
- about 33
- orange shake 56
- and pear shake 33

Cocktail
- peach melba 20
- tutti-frutti 53
- white fruit 23

Coconut
- about 14
- mango, drink 14

Coffee, about 54

Cucumber(s)
- about 47
- icy, dill drink 47

Abbreviations
tsp = teaspoon
tbsp = tablespoon

Dill, icy cucumber drink 47

Drink(s)
- apple and elderberry 24
- banana and yogurt 38
- cherry buttermilk 36
- icy cucumber dill 47
- kiwi and grapefruit with mint 18
- mango and coconut 14
- persimmon and orange 26
- pineapple and yogurt 41
- tomato andavocado 44

Elderberry(ies)
- about 24
- apple, drink 24

Fruit
- about 10
- cocktail, white 23
- seasonal calendar 11

Grapefruit, kiwi drink with mint 18
Grapes, about 53

Herb, carrot shake 48

Kiwi
- about 18
- and avocado mix 22
- and grapefruit drink with mint 18

Lime
- about 57
- shake, tangy 57

Mango(es)
- about 43
- and carrot mix 43
- and coconut drink 14

Melon(s)
- about 29
- shake 29

Mocha banana dream 54

Nut(s)
- about 37
- apple, shake 37

Orange
- chocolate, shake 56
- papaya, shake 17
- persimmon, drink 26

Papaya
- about 17
- orange, shake 17

Peach(es)
- about 20
- melba cocktail 20

Pear, chocolate shake 33
Peppers, about 46

Persimmon(s)
- about 26
- and orange drink 26

Pineapple
- about 41
- and yogurt drink 41
- strawberry, mix 16

Power week eating plan 8–9

Protein
- eat with little or no fat 6
- powder 7
- the power fuel 2–3

Raspberry(ies)
about 58
and poppy seed cream 58

Shake
apple and nut 37
apricot and almond 30
berry-cherry 40
blackcurrant and banana 27
C-packed blueberry 34
carrot and herb 48
chocolate orange 56
chocolate and pear 33
melon 29
papaya and orange 17
spicy vegetable 46
tangy lime 57

Smoothie, berry 13
Spinach, celeriac, flip 51

Strawberry(ies)
about 16
and pineapple mix 16

Tomato(es)
about 44
and avocado drink 44

Vanilla, about 56
Vegetable, shake, spicy 46

Yogurt
banana, drink 38
pineapple drink 41

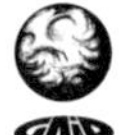

First published in the UK by Gaia Books Ltd, 20 High St, Stroud, GL5 1AZ

Registered at 66 Charlotte Street London W1T 4QE
Originally published under the title FOREVER YOUNG: Fitneß-Drinks

Translated in association with Silverback Books, Inc, US.

Editorial: Katherine Pate
Nutritional Advisor: Lorna Rhodes

Printed in Thailand

ISBN: 1-85675 103 1
A catalogue record of this book is available in the British Library.

Dr. Ulrich Strunz studied nuclear physics and medicine in Germany and abroad. He has performed research and published various works on the hormonal control of bodily functions (almost 100 scientific publications). He is currently a practising internist and ortho-molecular doctor and a personal physician to competitive and non-competitive athletes. At the age of 45, Strunz started participating in extreme sports and is now a world-class, ultra-triathlete in his age group.

Dr. Strunz holds fitness seminars and also writes books on the subject.

Caution
The techniques and recipes in this book are to be used at the reader's sole discretion and risk. Always consult a doctor before beginning a new eating plan or if in doubt about a medical condition.

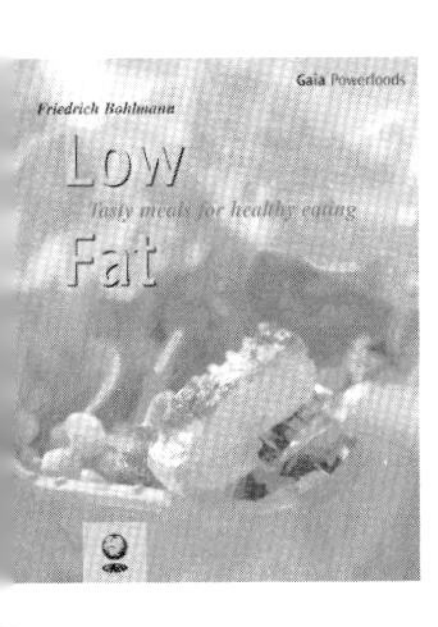

LOW FAT

Tasty meals for healthy eating

Friedrich Bohlmann

£5.99

ISBN 1 85675 113 9

Stay slim, healthy and full of vitality with quick, easy and yummy recipes to satisfy a healthy appetite.

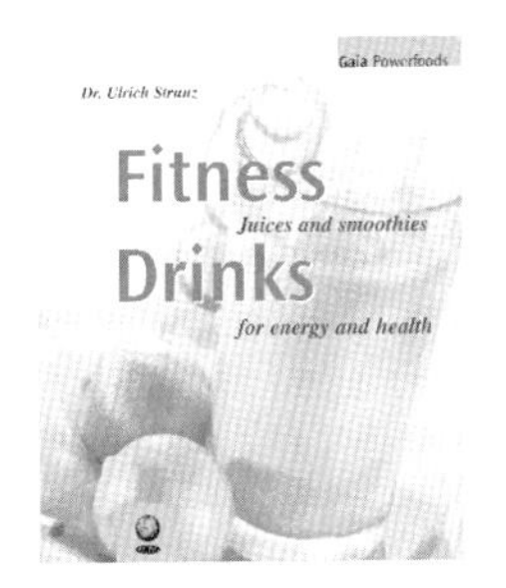

FITNESS DRINKS

Juices and smoothies for energy and health

Dr Ulrich Strunz

£5.99

ISBN 1 85675 103 1

Delicious recipes for protein-packed power drinks rich in essential vitamins and minerals.

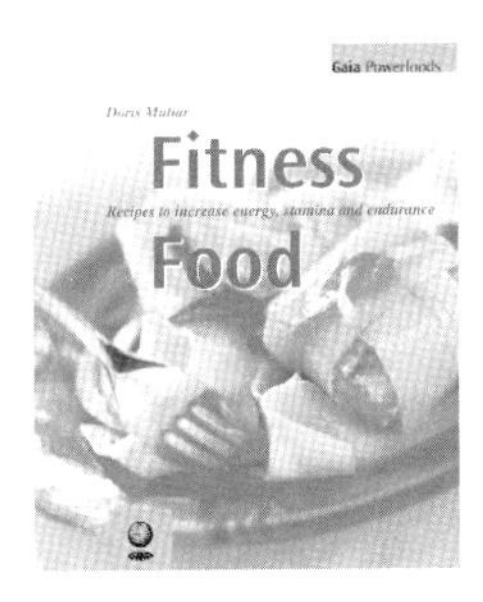

FITNESS FOOD

Recipes to increase energy, stamina and endurance

Doris Muliar

£5.99

ISBN 1 85675 167 8

No more lethargy and exhaustion. Healthy food for power, conditioning and performance during exercise and afterwards.

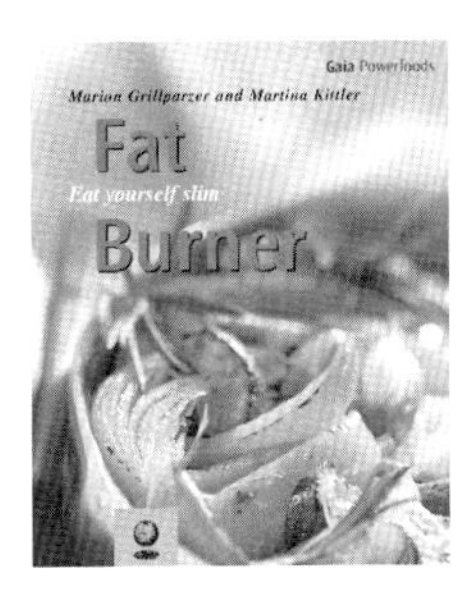

FAT BURNER

Eat yourself slim

Marion Grillparzer and Martina Kittler

£5.99

ISBN 1 85675 108 2

How to eat well and lose weight. Delicious foods that burn away excess fat and make you feel fantastic.

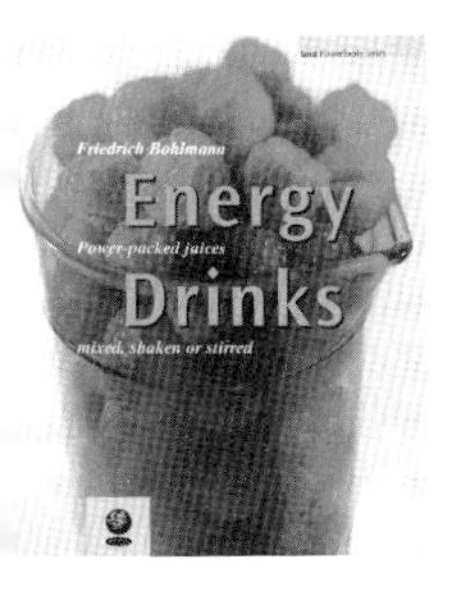

ENERGY DRINKS

Power-packed juices, mixed, shaken or stirred

Friedrich Bohlmann

£5.99

ISBN 1 85675 140 6

Fresh juices packed full of goodness for vitality and health.

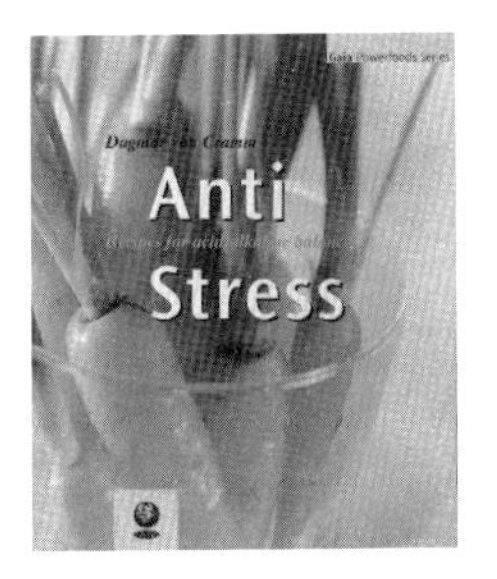

ANTI STRESS

Recipes for acid-alkaline balance

Dagmar von Cramm

£4.99

ISBN 1 85675 155 4

A balanced diet to reduce stress levels, maximise immunity and help you keep fit.

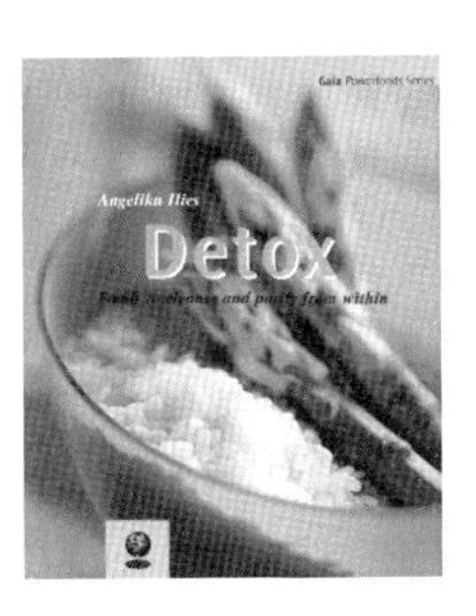

DETOX

Foods to cleanse and purify from within

Angelika Ilies

£5.99

ISBN 1 85675 150 3

Detoxify your body as part of your daily routine by eating nutritional foods that have cleansing properties.

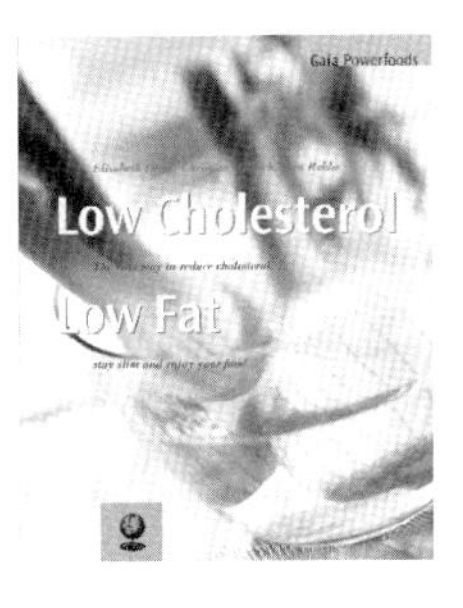

LOW CHOLESTEROL - LOW FAT

The easy way to reduce cholesterol, stay slim and enjoy your food

Döpp, Willrich and Rebbe

£4.99

ISBN 1 85675 166 X

Stay fit, slim and healthy with easy-to-prepare gourmet feasts.

To order the books featured on this page call 01453 752985, fax 01453 752987 with your credit/debit card details, or send a cheque made payable to Gaia Books to Gaia Books Ltd., 20 High Street, Stroud, Glos., GL5 1AZ.
e-mail: gaiapub@dircon.co.uk or visit our website www.gaiabooks.co.uk

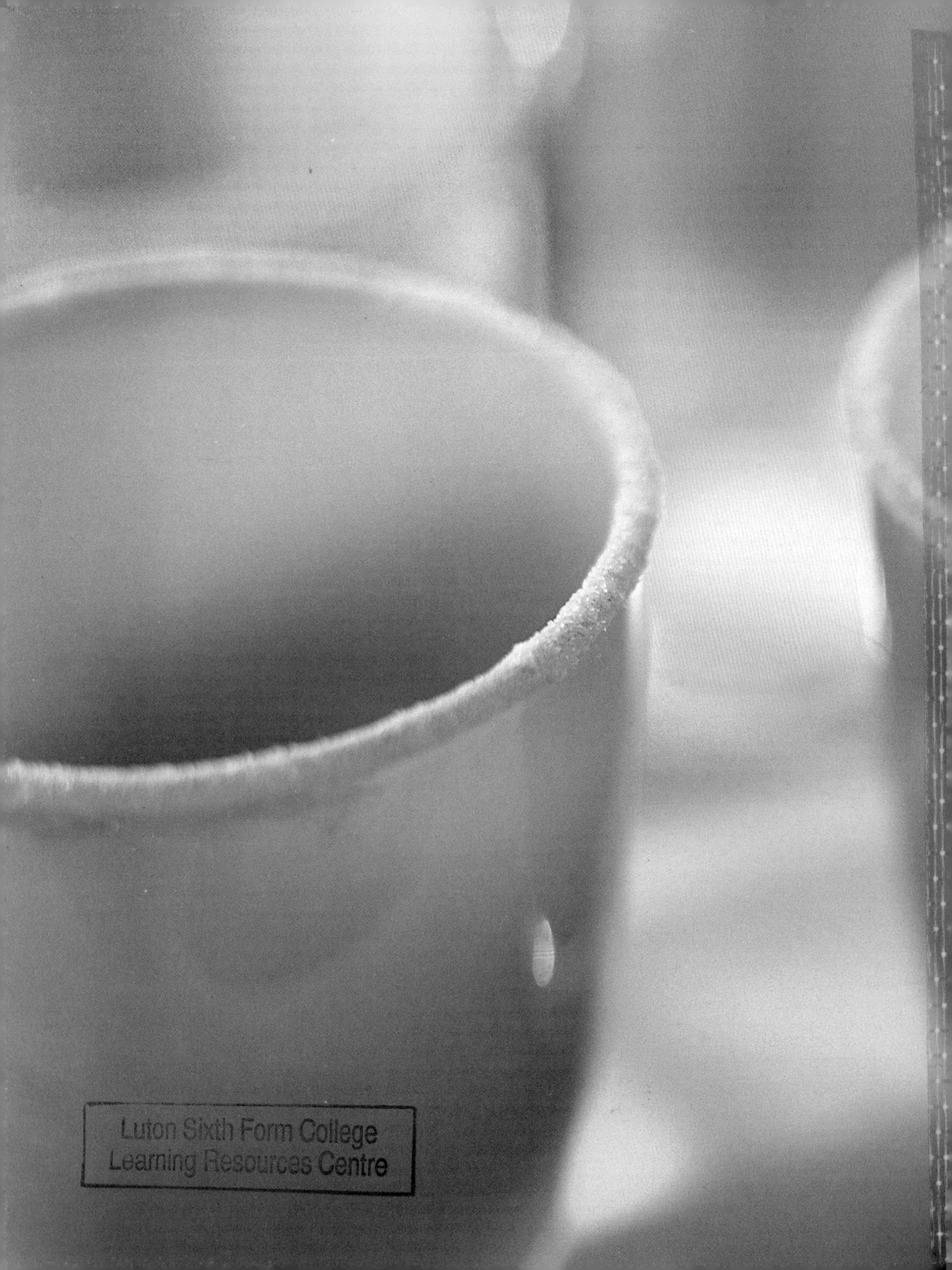